"In the 15th century the world was dominated by India, China and the Middle East. Maybe we are going to go back to the future."

Max Burger-Calderon,
Chairman of Apax Partners Asia

Acknowledgements

Thank you to everybody who agreed to be interviewed for this book. An extended list appears at the end of the text. There are a number of other people who have provided support during the past 18 months to whom I would like to give special mention:

Sarah Cook for her help in researching the ruling and merchant families; David Cairns for his project management skills and all my colleagues at Bladonmore – especially Nicolas Bruel and Grant Murgatroyd – who gave texture to the core story.

I would also like to thank my partner, Lauren, for her advice and encouragement.

And finally, I would like to dedicate the book to my grandparents, Jane and Harry.

Contents

First Impressions

It's 6 a.m. at Jeddah's international airport terminal. The Egyptian man next to me, who has flown in from the United States, is having his bags searched by the customs officers. They find five DVDs. These include Hollywood films such as *Alexander*, the historical drama of the Greek leader, and a boxed set of *Desperate Housewives*, the popular US television series.

The besuited gentleman from Cairo looks forlorn and says: "I appreciate the content may not pass the censors. I just want to get home. Keep the DVDs." The customs officer looks up at him and smiles warmly: "What do you mean? We have joined the World Trade Organisation. I just want to make sure they are originals and not counterfeit. Enjoy them."

The head of investments for one of Kuwait's leading trading families pulls on another cigarette – his fifth since our meeting started 30 minutes ago. "Last week one of the shareholders told me about an investment opportunity that he thought we should back," he says.

He takes a puff and continues: "Two days later, I was contacted by the chairman and told it was a good investment opportunity. The reason I was late for our meeting was that I spent 40 minutes writing a memo as to why we should not invest in the company. I gave four reasons why I did not think it was a good investment," he continues matter-of-factly.

"Sure, if the shareholders want to invest their personal money, they can, but I know that they will not use the trading firm to make the investment. They respect my judgement and my role. How many companies in the West would bring that level of governance to what they do? I am an employee who is reliant on their sponsorship to stay, but I also realise that I could be fired tomorrow. What I do know is that the funds of the company will not be used to make that investment. Contrary to what others may generalise, they could not deny that these are anything but advanced corporate governance procedures."

"Welcome to Applebee's," smiles the Thai waiter. Yet another franchise operation from the US making money by serving faux Mexican food to a hungry Riyadh crowd. Thumbing through my drinks options, I note that massive margaritas are absent from the menu.

It is 2.58 p.m. and darkness descends. Blinds come down, doors are closed and Saudi locals smile knowingly as they tuck into their chocolate brownies. From the outside, Applebee's appears closed for business, but from the inside business goes on for both the restaurant and the 50 Saudi business people who are cutting deals over their coffee and cake.

The meeting in Dubai's Media City is brought to order. The Indian account director is overseeing a project for his Finnish client. He turns to his colleague: "Faoud, my Lebanese friend, what do you think?" The man from Beirut shrugs his shoulders, refusing to be drawn. Francesca, who has moved from Rome to develop her career, sits up and makes her recommendation. Her colleague from Ireland nods in agreement. And so ends yet another example of the entrepôt in action, a truly heterogeneous mix of people, who have made Dubai their new home in their quest to build new roots.

These four anecdotes are told as they happened. Each provides further evidence of what everyone understands to be true. Reform is charging ahead and the Middle East[1] region is in the midst of an economic revolution. The fundamental requirement to generate sustainable employment opportunities is its single greatest challenge. It is underpinned by a demographic urgency that is driving change in the region's education systems in a bid to create a globally competitive workforce.

So what is the hypothesis of this book?

The Middle East has a rich cultural and historical identity that can trace its way back through the ages. It would be easy to pinpoint the key moments and people contributing to the commercial development of the Middle East. From the fictional world of *Sinbad the Sailor* to the modern era of Sheikh Rashid bin Saeed Al Maktoum, the region has been a hub for commerce and trade, providing a key path between Europe to the West and Asia to the East.

The Arab people are not a homogeneous group yet commercial and trading nous is an inherent feature of many. It is this trading gene that launched so many of the great merchant families and built the basis of more than 500 significant trading groups across the region. While this book celebrates their efforts and puts the spotlight on a number, it is not here to record history.

In fact, it argues that it is actually a much more recent event – September 11, 2001 – that marks the key date in terms of the fuelling of the development of the Middle East as a commercial region in its own right. Countless articles, books and programmes have been written on its impact.

But this text believes that the response of the West in general and the US in particular to this barbaric act of terrorism has led many in the Arab world to question whether they should continue to invest so wholeheartedly on an international scale. The protectionist furore over the 2006 acquisition by DP World of P&O UK, leading to the forced sale of its US assets, is just the latest example of why Gulf capital is being repatriated, driving the determination to create a vibrant economic hub in its own right.

1   Israel remains a key part of the Middle East. It is officially recognised by many Arab states and has informal communication channels with others. The economic ties between its companies and those in the Arab world are growing. However, for the sake of this book, the Middle East does not make reference to or include Israel. Israel has its own dynamic venture capital and private equity business, boosted by its links with the United States, and there are a number of books on the subject already. Desert Capitalists is focused principally on the Gulf and the Levant region

Emirates like Dubai are not alone in living off the borrowed time of black gold. As oil is pumped, the region needs fresh initiatives and is working exceptionally hard at this. Dubai is a brilliant example of a national private equity firm in action. It was the national port that has grown internationally via acquisition into a global group, albeit one that has now had to dispose of its US assets. This is but one example of a ruling family's vision turning opportunity into commercial reality.

If capital from the oil-rich Gulf is not welcome overseas, is it any surprise that it is being invested locally, spawning a new generation of financiers, with ever greater ideas and schemes to generate a new generation of returns? Arab investors are backing the markets and the people they know and trust. Coupled with unprecedented oil prices, this is a boom unparalleled in history.

Consequently we are living in the era of *Desert Capitalists*, where the very people who are able to generate the necessary employment opportunities, and who treat globalisation as an opportunity rather than a curse, are to be found in business rather than politics.

They operate comfortably within the context of political structures and rules propagated by the ruling families. These people – manifested through the next generation of merchant families and private equity investors – are the very ones with the sense and understanding to confront the challenge of regional unemployment and poverty throughout the region.

This text argues that the region is set to enjoy an unprecedented amount of deal activity over the next decade. Privatisations driven by governments that recognise the need to be regulators of businesses rather than owners, flotations by merchant families of certain assets, and a number of expatriate businessmen wanting to return home, will drive the deal flow. Opportunities will beget opportunities.

These people are a totally different breed from the herd like investors who have fuelled a bubble in the regional stock markets during the past two years. The spring 2006 correction – this book does not believe it was more than that – may have been presented in the local media as a crash but it is just another step in the journey of these developing markets.

If it leads to individual retail investors halting their foolish rush to give up day jobs and become traders – stories of which have filled a number of late night radio phone-ins – then it can only be a good thing. Ultimately the markets need to mature and the correction will be seen as a step in that direction.

Underlying it all, however, is the biggest challenge of all: generating enough new jobs to support the demographic surge of the Middle East. This book argues that economics now takes priority over politics. The way ahead is to empower the business leaders of today and tomorrow to go for growth. They have more practical answers than the army, the politicians and a legion of economists and sociologists.

The required solutions are to be found in the offices of business rather than in the political labyrinth. Of course it is impossible for Egypt, Saudi Arabia, the UAE and the wider region to develop economically without the consent of the ruling families and elites. It would be naïve to say otherwise.

But there are genuine opportunities and reasons for hope. Blue ribbon investors like the famous Carlyle Group of the United States are poised to enter the region. They are being aided by the arrival of international investment banks, such as Morgan Stanley and Goldman Sachs, which will bring a raft of new products to an interested audience growing used to an increasingly sophisticated regional network of banks and finance houses.

Competition forces the domestic operators to become smarter and think through how they can respond to the changing undulations of the market. They may have the relationships, which count for so much, but in a global environment, everyone's expectations rise.

Consequently, now is the appropriate time to pause and reflect on who the *Desert Capitalists* are, where they have come from and where they are going. Taken together, they offer the best prospect for finding the answers to the most difficult questions faced by the region.

Finally, this book is a snapshot of a time that raises questions to be answered over the coming years. I seek your forgiveness for any errors – they are mine – and am grateful to the generosity of spirit that accompanied me wherever I went. Thank you.

Richard Rivlin, Monday April 17th, 2006

Foreword

Shafik Gabr is chairman and managing director of Artoc Group for Investment & Development. He is also a founding member and chairman of the Arab Business Council of the World Economic Forum.

The eyes of the world have been on the Middle East for much of this decade – a consequence of September 11, global energy requirements and the unfolding situations in Iraq, Palestine and Israel. Our politicians are under the international spotlight and have huge responsibilities on their shoulders. But theirs is not a responsibility to be borne alone.

Our business leaders need to step forward and demonstrate a commitment to reforming our companies, making them more competitive and thus generating the employment opportunities that our region craves. This was the context surrounding the launch of the Arab Business Council.

The sense of urgency is acute, especially when unemployment rates average 15 per cent across the region and reach 30 per cent for those under 24. To keep these rates without change, 80 million jobs need to be created between today and 2019. This requires a job creation rate of 4 per cent annually, which has not been achieved anywhere in the world in the past century. But that does not mean it is impossible, provided "out of the box" creative policies are pursued.

The history of the Arab Business Council can be traced back to the August 2002 World Economic Forum's *'Arab World Competitiveness Report'* which starkly demonstrated how poor the competitive position of the Arab world is. Its shocking figures prompted the formation of an Arab Business Council in 2003 and our mission now, as it was then, can be summed up in two words: *Reform* and *Competitiveness.*

Given the economic reality of a global, knowledge-based economy, the Arab world needs much deeper cooperation among the leading voices of the Arab business sector if it is to compete successfully.

This is a perspective shared by all our members, a number of whom have gone on and taken key roles in driving the regional reform process. For instance former members of the ABC include: Amr Dabbagh, who is now Governor of the Saudi Arabian General Investment Authority; Rachid Mohammed Rachid, as Minister of Trade and Industry of Egypt; Sheikha Lubna Al Qasimi, as Minister of Economy and Planning of the UAE; Sharif Ali Zu'bi, as Minister of Industry and Trade of Jordan; Mohammed Mansour as Minister of Transport of Egypt; and Hatem El-Gabaly as Minister of Health of Egypt. This is a genuinely promising step towards a greater role for the business community in bringing about economic reform and competitiveness in the region.

Council Members have developed a *Blueprint for Economic Reform* and helped launch the first National Competitiveness Council in Egypt. These councils gather leaders from private sector organisations, governments, NGOs and academics that seek national answers to national problems and focus principally on monitoring, benchmarking and evaluating key economic, political and social indicators, and also propose policy recommendations.

We live in an era when there is a battle of ideas unfolding across the region. Readers of international news media are used to seeing articles that are focused on demonstrating the differences between East and West. Regional business leaders must contribute to the process and one key theme to develop is the need for business in the region to stop working hand in glove with government and start working side by side – with governments, NGOs, community leaders and international organizations – towards a brighter future for the region.

Following a successful launch in Egypt, other Councils have been launched in Bahrain and Kuwait to a positive response and constructive cooperation between Governments and the NCCs.

There have also been a number of discussions with Asian business leaders, the G-8, the OECD and a variety of US groups – including Congress, the Administration, the media, think tanks and NGOs – to ensure that stronger links are forged on behalf of the Arab business community.

The protagonists of this debate are likely to be the very people – the merchant families and investors – that this text argues are the key hopes for generating sustainable employment opportunities. The Arab Business Council is not a political organisation but it believes that company leaders do have an obligation that goes far beyond the bottom line to assist in developing the region.

One of the many special features of *Desert Capitalists* is the author's ability to demonstrate that our region is not homogenous. We may speak the same language but we are very different and, consequently, there is a real need to promote regional and national ideas that are grounded in practical realities. It is impossible to undertake reform – building the necessary institutions and developing a sustainable future – without ensuring things progress brick by brick, step by step.

The Arab Business Council is a catalyst for change and a source of new ideas and fresh thinking. Over the next three years we expect to develop a number of new Competitiveness Councils across the region work in partnership with governments and international organizations to eradicate illiteracy and improve education, promote a series of new ideas and ensure that the media – locally, regionally and internationally – is fully aware of the opportunities and latent talent in our region.

Business remains the strongest force for generating employment opportunities and building a stronger future for our region. So I commend this book for highlighting the trends, institutions and individuals who are leading change in our region. I might not agree with all of its content, but at its heart it provides a fresh message for our times. I applaud my fellow *Desert Capitalists* for the work they have done to date but now encourage them to go further and open the way for the next generation of leaders to emerge.

Only when leaders with a vision emerge – backed up a constituency of support and institutions capable of managing change – will our region be able to compete globally.

Shafik Gabr, April 2006

Chapter 1

The role for capital in the Middle East

TACKLING UNEMPLOYMENT: THE NUMBER ONE PRIORITY

The Middle East is running out of time to find sustainable solutions for under-employment and its ugly twin – unemployment. From the chaotic streets of Cairo to the dusty lanes of Jeddah into the deep of Muscat, it is top of the agenda. The unemployment crisis demands an urgent and sustainable response from the ruling families and governments in the region. Who knows what the tipping point was – the question is no longer whether to reform and restructure, but how fast do we turn things around and which process do we use? Moreover, how do we sustain employment growth?

Bassem Awadallah, former Finance and Economics Minister of Jordan, who is in the process of launching a new regional investment bank, says: "The facts are simple. There are 70 million people under the age of 30 in the region. Millions of them need jobs." Visitors to the Gulf cannot help but be dazzled by the wealth that is in the region. The raw power of Saudi Arabia, the construction boom in Qatar and Kuwait, the scale of ambition in the UAE and the growth in Oman means the Gulf is destined to become one of the most advanced economic regions in the world. The sheer professionalism of this area leaves much of the West standing in its tracks, and the opportunities for people with energy and enterprise make it one of the crucibles of capitalism in the 21st century.

However, the gap between the classes is vast. It is very difficult to get up-to-date facts about the scale of unemployment in the region. John Sfakianakis, chief regional economist at Samba Bank in Saudi Arabia, says: "Oil does not generate jobs. It is capital intensive, not labour intensive. So we can have high growth rates, but we are not generating enough jobs."

However, there is a stark difference between the grandness of the hotel lobbies of Riyadh's Al Faisaliah and Dubai's Emirates Towers, and the large swathes of desolate land in between. There remain large parts, even within the Gulf and the wider Levant region, that are experiencing huge levels of poverty. One does not need to stray far from the tourist tracks in Egypt or Morocco, let alone Palestine or Libya, to see how polarised wealth is in the region.

The rate of unemployment is extremely high throughout the region. At the same time, the labour force has increased at a faster pace than anywhere else in the world, thanks to soaring demographic growth. However, behind the construction boom are some weak economic growth statistics. During the last two decades, while East Asia was growing at a yearly rate of 5.8 per cent, per capita income did not grow by even one per cent in the Middle East. For example, the Levant has performed particularly poorly and many people are no better off than they were 20 years ago.

According to Christiaan Poortman, vice-president of the World Bank for the Middle East and North Africa Region, the region needs to create around 100 million jobs by the year 2020[1] in order to make a serious impact on unemployment levels. Never before has a region of this size had to create so many jobs in such a short period of time.

The challenge is clearly daunting, particularly since recent demand for labour has been sluggish at best. In addition, such labour needs can seldom be accommodated domestically because local education does not provide employers with the quality of staff they require.

The managing partner of a professional services firm in the Gulf says: "I want to hire locals. It is what the government encourages. But do locals want to work? The work ethic is not as it needs to be."

The double-edged sword is that you have a large population of young people who are educated enough to be put off by manual jobs, but at the same time lack the skills required by white-collar growth companies. This is paired with the fact that the local economies do not favour labour-intensive industries.

ECONOMIC LIBERALISATION: OPENING BORDERS

Majid Saif Al Ghurair, chief executive of Al Ghurair Group, noted at the 2005 World Economic Forum in Jordan that the Middle East needs to open its borders to develop industries that generate employment at a significant rate. Of course, the demographic situation makes this need particularly acute. Essentially, governments have no choice but to deliver accelerated economic growth simply to maintain standards of living. Over recent years, these have fallen. But they can't afford to fall further.

Historically, local governments have shied away from much-needed structural reforms and have favoured short-term measures, bloating the public sector and hiring employees in this area. Over the long term, however, this is not a viable solution.

According to official unemployment figures for 2004, Egypt saw levels reach 10.9 per cent; 15 per cent in Jordan; and 18 per cent in Lebanon, although actual rates were estimated closer to 30 per cent. Governments know that hungry and frustrated young people are the most likely recruits for extremist Islamic movements, which is another factor behind the economic liberalisation sweeping the region.

It gets worse. The percentage of people living below the poverty line is substantial – reaching 16.7 per cent in Egypt; 30 per cent in Jordan; and 28 per cent in Lebanon. One in five inhabitants of the Middle East continues to live on less than $2 a day, according to World Bank figures.

---

1   Speech to the World Economic Forum on Infrastructure Challenges, Jordan, May 2005

Meanwhile, across the entire region, the number of urban dwellers is expected to grow from 135 million to more than 350 million over the next two decades. Such rapid demographic movement always causes problems, particularly surrounding infrastructure with its domino impact on the provision of housing, sewage, hospital and schooling.

Pascal Roger from the utility leader Suez, provider of water and electricity services to much of the developing world and a key figure at the World Economic Forum, explains that often utility projects are rendered economically non-viable because the population could not afford the price of the service. He says: "This is where the private sector must be creative and partner with local governments, so they can work together on long-term profitable schemes."

The World Bank estimates the investment needs of the region will amount to tens of billions of dollars over the next ten years.[2] But where will that capital come from?

Arif Naqvi, founder of UAE-based private equity firm Abraaj Capital and fellow member of the World Economic Forum, says: "Private companies will need a fair environment to operate in. But if governments leave them alone to get on with business, they can generate wealth and jobs, as well as provide much needed investment capital."

Ideally, then, governments, local private investors and foreign companies would work in unison to deliver the capital and skills required to boost economic growth, tackle unemployment and develop infrastructure. But, September 11 notwithstanding, a significant amount of local wealth is held offshore. In addition, the Levant attracts a tiny share of foreign direct investments; and, apart from oil companies, large Western multinationals shun the region. In other words, the Middle East has to confront a huge challenge.

When looking at Egypt, Jordan and Lebanon, four main factors restrain economic growth and call for further liberalisation: the omnipotence of the public sector, which sidelines the private sector and discourages entrepreneurs; tax regimes that prohibit growth; complex and opaque regulations that fail to stem corruption; and immature legal systems that are unable to settle commercial conflicts.

Capital has a huge role to play in helping to turn these countries around. They have some of the highest rates of unemployment in the world, yet lack the wherewithal to improve their circumstances. It is a truly daunting state of affairs. To gain some idea of what will have to be achieved if the Arab world is to make any serious progress, it is worth taking a look at some of the economies of East Asia. Over the past 20 years, many of these economies have enjoyed spectacular economic growth and massive job creation, notching up some of the highest rates of sustained employment growth in modern history. In China, there was a 40 per cent increase in the total number of jobs between 1980 and 2000.

South Korea, which has climbed dramatically up the economic ladder to become the world's tenth largest economy, saw employment grow by almost 60 per cent over the same period. But the best performer over the same two decades is Malaysia, which was able to increase the number of jobs by almost 90 per cent. Over the coming two decades, the whole of the Arab region will have to perform better than East Asia's best performer if it is to cope with the current and future population explosion.[3]

GOVERNANCE: THE RULING CRITERIA

In recent years, development agencies have come to understand that driving economic growth is considerably more complicated than they had thought. "Economists used to think that if you brought inflation into line, then everything else would fall into play," says Augusto Lopez-Carlos, chief economist and director of the Global Competitiveness Programme of the World Economic Forum. "But we have now realised the importance of institutional factors, such as waste, efficiency and even-handedness."

The implications are clear, with regard to the Middle East. And they can be neatly summed up by the World Bank. More than two decades ago, economists working at the Bank – a body that is expressly forbidden from taking political factors into consideration – hit upon the word 'governance' to describe the conditions required to create sustainable development.

Ismail Serageldin, a former vice-president of the World Bank writing in the "Arab World Competitiveness Report", explains the thinking: "Governance was not about whether the system was two-party, multi-party, parliamentary or presidential – that would have been overly political – but rather that good governance was about transparency, pluralism, participation, the rule of law and the free flow of information. Later, democracy, respect for human rights and gender equality became widely accepted as key components of good governance. To these nine characteristics, a tenth may be added: a learning environment that nurtures innovation and respects youth."

Failure may have catastrophic consequences for one of the world's least stable areas. It is this issue that is seen by many commentators as the key factor behind a willingness by the ruling families and leaders to instigate the economic reforms that will boost enterprise and employment opportunities within the region. As a central premise in this book, now is the time for private equity to truly assist in the economic development of the region.

There are a number of trade and finance ministers throughout the region who are like-minded in their belief that this is the only way forward. From Rachid Mohammed Rachid, Egypt's Minister for Trade, to Saudi Arabia's Minister of Finance, HE Dr Ibrahim Al-Assaf, and others beyond those borders, there is a common bond in making the leap forward together. Much rests on the shoulders of these individuals, and their ability to drive through reforms in countries where not everybody is convinced of their merits.

3   Arif Naqvi speech to Terrapin conference on private equity in the Middle East, September 2005

For instance, in Saudi Arabia the ruling family may appoint senior members of the clergy, but they have no direct day-to-day control of the 600-plus judges that run the Sharia courts. The judges provide the backbone of the Saudi legal system and do not operate with the same vision as that of the reformers.

THE REGION'S RULING FAMILIES

Pan-Arabism has historically been hanging on to romantic optimism rather than practical on-the-ground realities. Clamouring for political supremacy isn't on the agenda, either, as the region seems more focused on increasing the individual wealth of its component parts.

Syria and Iran, two of the command economies in the region, have their own agendas currently manifested through their individual stand-offs with parts of the United Nations. But by and large, when it comes to financial security, the region's leaders acknowledge their domestic responsibilities.

The ruling families and elites maintain absolute power over their jurisdiction. Consequently, any text that attempts to provide a perspective on economics in the region and the emergence of new forces must step back, pause and recognise the role played by the ruling families. Where state ownership begins and ruling family holdings end is a debatable issue. Is it the Al Saud family that owns 70 per cent of SABIC, the stock market darling of Saudi Arabia, or is it the Saudi government?

These are the individuals who ultimately make the decisions about the pace of change. However, as they have told us, it is never as simple as stopping and starting the engine of reform.

There is a separate text to be produced on the royal families and their members as business people in their own right. They consist of literally hundreds of regional members, each with their own private offices and the ability to invest significant sums domestically, regionally and internationally. Some research has estimated the number of people in the Middle East with direct royal connections as being as many as 40,000. These individuals are critical to the long-term development of the region and it is one of the weaknesses of this book that it has not been able to access as many of the families listed below as it would like. This will be a challenge for the second edition.

Country	Ruling individual or family/Year started in power	
Algeria	President: Abdelaziz Bouteflika	1999
Bahrain	King: Sheikh Hamad bin Isa al-Khalifah	1999
Egypt	President: Hosni Mubarak	1981
Iran	Supreme leader: Ayatollah Ali Khamenei	1989
Iraq	Interim president: Jalal Talabani	2005
Jordan	His Majesty King Abdullah II bin Al Hussein	1999
Kuwait	Emir: Sheikh Sabah al-Ahmed al-Jaber	2006
Lebanon	President: General Emile Lahoud	1998
Libya	Head of State: Colonel Muammar Abu Minyar al-Qaddafi	1969
Morocco	His Majesty King Mohammed VI	1999
Oman	Sultan, prime minister: Qaboos bin Said Al Said	1970
Qatar	Emir: Sheikh Hamad bin Khalifa al-Thani	1995
Saudi Arabia	King Abdullah Bin-Abd-al-Aziz Al Saud	2005
Syria	President: Bashar al-Assad	2000
Tunisia	President: Zine El Abidine Ben Ali	1987
UAE	President, ruler of Abu Dhabi: Sheikh Khalifa bin Zayed	2004

The Marathon Men: the top for longevity

Libya	Head of State: Colonel Muammar Abu Minyar al-Qaddafi	1969
Oman	Sultan, prime minister: Qaboos Bin Said Al Said	1970
Egypt	President: Hosni Mubarak	1981
Tunisia	President: Zine El Abidine Ben Ali	1987
Iran	Supreme leader: Ayatollah Ali Khamenei	1989

New Blood: fresh members of the Middle East top table

Kuwait	Emir: Sheikh Sabah al-Ahmed al-Jaber al-Sabah	2006
Iraq	Interim president: Jalal Talabani	2005
Saudi Arabia	King Abdullah Bin-Abd-al-Aziz Al Saud	2005
UAE	President, ruler of Abu Dhabi: Sheikh Khalifa bin Zayed	2004
Syria	President: Bashar al-Assad	2000

Source: www.bbc.co.uk + www.bladonmore.com

The sheer nature of these states dictates that different family members will have varying objectives and agendas. Consequently reforms that one branch wish to pursue may not get past another. It is, as one member of the Saudi court said, "about wriggling forward rather than going in a straight line". This is an important point. The ruling families have access to the brightest minds in the world and are fully aware of the implications of globalisation, coupled with their own demographic issues. However, there is only so much speed at which they can reform their own nations.

Prince Fahad Bin Abdullah from Saudi Arabia says: "The pace that the government adopts has the consensus of the family, business people and prominent people within society. There is no conflict within the family. There must be cohesiveness between the steps we take and our people. Some believe we are going at the right pace and others think we should go faster. You do not want the vehicle to accelerate at its maximum pace or go too slowly to create a traffic jam."

Wriggling forward is never a simple task as it involves navigating the forces of both tradition and modernity. It is no wonder that privately many will emphasise the responsibility that falls on the shoulders of business leaders. This is not because they are abrogating their tasks. Instead they are delicately balancing the needs of all constituencies including the religious leaders who have their own agenda.

What follows are mini-profiles of the four key regional economies: Saudi Arabia, Egypt, UAE and Qatar. The Middle East resembles a jumbo jet and these four nations are akin to individual engines that are fuelling its forward movements. At any one time they may not all be going perfectly, but there is enough strength from the others to carry the direction of the plane. Of course there are many other economies in the region which are significant. Kuwait, for instance, includes some of the most powerful families in the whole region and is of key strategic importance. But in terms of where we are at today, it is these named four that are the engine of the region, so it makes sense to examine where they are at. Of these four, the powerhouse of the region undoubtedly remains Saudi Arabia.

THE ECONOMIC ENGINE: INSIDE SAUDI ARABIA

Fawaz Al-Alamy is a busy man. The special adviser to the Minister of Commerce and Industry has recently completed the negotiations for Saudi Arabia's entry into the World Trade Organisation. The negotiator-in-chief for the region now has bilateral agreements to make with the EU, China, Brazil and the United States. His grasp of economic detail and statistics is mesmerising.

"The World Bank has just released its annual review ranking the world's best environments in which to invest. We came 38th, which was the highest Arab state, and we beat the likes of France, Italy and Portugal," he beams.

In 2004, Saudi Arabia came a lowly 76th. Its spurt up the World Bank's league table characterises a shift in emphasis that is emerging from the country. Objective observers might suggest it should be higher. This is a country that has been politically stable for much of the past century, enjoys the advantages of being the leading source of oil in the world, 60 per cent of its population are under 18 and it has a low tax environment for international businesses. However, few international business people yearn to spend time in the country, preferring to base themselves in the less culturally conservative business centres of Bahrain, Kuwait or Dubai.

High oil prices helped generate a budget surplus of more than $50 billion during 2005 and there is no reason why the number will not be equally high in 2006 or 2007. If the Middle East region is viewed as a turbine for global trade, then the Kingdom of Saudi Arabia is the key component that mobilises the machine. Its stock market accounts for practically half the value of stocks listed on the 15 Arab stock markets registered with the Arab Monetary Fund.

However, the Kingdom is simultaneously blessed and cursed. Its blessing – oil reserves unlike any other in the world – has been a catalyst for its curse – a lack of efficiency and depth of domestic talent to drive the region's engine forward.

Entry to the WTO is likely to be a seminal moment for the country and the region. According to Brad Bourland, chief economist at Samba Bank in Saudi Arabia, "There is no single agreement or commitment to the WTO that dramatically affects the economy. Rather, it is the cumulative impact of the hundreds of incremental changes that is broadly positive for growth. This is already demonstrated by accelerating growth of the non-oil private sector over the years of negotiation."

He adds that, from 1990-1995, private sector GDO growth averaged 1.7 per cent per year. From 2000-2005, growth accelerated to average five per cent per year. The reform and trade liberalisation of the past decade, much attributable to the preparation for WTO membership, accounts for some of the higher growth rates. For the rest of this decade we believe private sector growth will range from six to eight per cent, in line with or above the sustainable organic rate of growth. In addition, WTO membership furthers several primary goals of economic policy – diversification of the economy away from oil, job creation for Saudis and the attraction of foreign investment.

In respect of this, Al-Alamy says: "We have three major challenges. Reduce our dependency on oil as a source of national income[4], generate jobs for Saudi nationals and ensure our GDP grows at a faster rate than our population."

The responsibility for reform may rest on the shoulders of government, but the execution will be passed to the private sector. The country is recognising the increased role of the private sector to generate employment opportunities.

Saudi Arabia is quickly developing three potentially international centres. Riyadh is the political nerve centre for both the Kingdom and arguably the region. Jeddah is rapidly developing as a commercial centre and has ambitions to become a hub for economics just as it is becoming a gateway to Mecca and Medina. Finally, Damman is now the oil capital of the world.

---

4   It accounts for 89 per cent of income according to the Ministry of Commerce & Industry

At a superficial level, there are many comparisons to be made with the United States. Both have vast continental land masses and house the elites on their Eastern and Western coasts, which are open to the influences of the wider world. They both have national elites who are exceptionally well educated, often internationally. But one has the Bible Belt and the other has the Koranic Core, which puts religion above all else. Even in Riyadh, in the heartland of the country, the atmosphere is much more austere than in the coastal regions.

Scratch the surface and the pace of reform becomes a dominant theme for discussion, advocated most prominently by the business elite, who are undoubtedly excited by what the entry to the World Trade Organisation actually means. But critics argue that the pace is not fast enough. There are factions within the ruling family that prohibit the opening of its borders solely to realise vast economic change. There's also the issue of initiating a more welcoming spirit to foreign executives, such as making entry into the country a little simpler and more pleasant.

Anthony Cordesman, a scholar at the Center for Strategic and International Studies in Washington, says: "King Abdullah has to take into account, like all the previous kings at least since Abdul Aziz, that there are other senior princes, tribal leaders and heads of important families. This is something that is often overlooked because of the tendency to translate the Saudi monarchy into Western terms or to see the absence of some kind of formally elected parliament as something that allows the king to operate freely."

In Saudi Arabia all paths ultimately lead to the royal family, so there is no point in reviewing the country without accessing the thinking of its number one family. It is large and extended with many members providing a variety of perspectives. Each is valuable in their own right and HH Prince Fahad Bin Abdullah is just a member of the extended grouping.

His roles extend to being Assistant Minister of Defence and Aviation and head of the Civil Aviation Authority. He is also a director of Saudi Arabian Airlines. Seen by many inside Saudi Arabia as a progressive force, he is determined to push the need for economic reform further up the agenda.

He believes that the principal focus must be on qualifying Saudi Arabia's population first and foremost and then concentrating on how they are employed.

He says: "It should have been done a long time ago. There are some success stories. Go and visit the Advanced Electronics Company, for instance, and see for yourself. In the past we stopped sending people abroad for education, but now we know that a diversified education is important. We are catching up. Last year 75,000 people applied for international education. More than 5,500 went to the United States and 2,700 went to the UK."

He believes that private enterprise has a huge responsibility to assist in the development of the country and wider region. "Saudi Arabia now accounts for 42 per cent of all the trade in the Arab world. Twenty years ago, 90,000 Saudis owned shares. Today, the number is 3.5 million.

As we develop our privatisation plans, that number could rise to eight million people who own shares. Saudi Arabia could become the hub for trade. In order for us to progress there is a lot of regulation that is being modified and initiated to meet the challenges. Last year we introduced 42 new business-friendly laws. For instance, laws related to intellectual property rights, such as the launch of the Capital Markets Authority, and patents."

Privately there are many in business who remain dissatisfied with the pace of reform in the region. In 1997 the government announced plans to privatise 20 major state assets. The process is based on corporatisation, then commercialisation and finally privatisation.

A good example is Saudi Arabian Airlines. "At the moment, we are in the process of corporatising the catering, cargo and airline operations of Saudi Arabian Airlines. These are three different businesses. We are working with international banks and consultants in getting this right," says Prince Fahad. In April 2006 it announced the appointment of BNP Paribas as the lead adviser for the flotation of Saudi Arabian Airlines, which is likely to become one of the most high profile listings of the region this year.

However, the message that a float such as this sends out has many nuances. Companies that want to operate to international standards need to recognise the terms demanded. That means best practice corporate governance standards and a recognition of the need to separate ownership from management.

The link between this and family businesses is obvious. He believes that the need to introduce best practice corporate governance is fundamental to the success of family businesses in the region. "The potential for family splits and disputes is a dangerous one. People could lose jobs. Businesses that should flourish might decay. So we must support moves to improve governance," he says, adding: "It is very important to have the economy driving politics, not the other way round."

The institutionalisation of best practice business and management, and the positive impact it could ultimately have, is a key driver for many in the Saudi elite. King Abdullah gave a speech in April 2006 when he stated explicitly: "The Kingdom cannot remain frozen while the world is changing around us," and vowed to move ahead with political and economic reforms.

Many look to SAGIA – the Saudi Arabian General Investment Authority – to provide guidance in this regard. It symbolises the importance that the government has given to private equity in the region and reinforces the viewpoint that private equity can be a developer of the private sector. For instance, SAGIA has sponsored a number of domestic funds including the Malaz $100 million ICT venture capital fund and Intel Capital's $50 million fund.

Dr Abdallah Dabbagh is president and chief executive of Saudi Arabian Mining, locally called Ma'aden, and seen by many as a manifestation of the changes unfolding in the country. He is a member of a very select club in Saudi Arabia. The informal network of future public company

CEOs carry the hopes and expectations of so many in the market and the country.

Currently Saudi Arabian Mining is a joint stock company which is owned in its entirety by the government. It has a stated objective of going private by December 2006. He says: "We have had a privatisation plan in place for some time to list on the Saudi Stock Exchange. It follows on from our restructuring a year ago and we now have JP Morgan in place to advise us on the flotation."

The business is expected to be valued at $2 billion with 50 per cent of the group's equity listed on the market. The Saudi government will retain the other 50 per cent with a view to diluting its holding over a three-year period.

Dabbagh's story is representative of many of the new generation of business leaders. "I am a geologist by background. I set up a contract research organisation from scratch but left when we got to 300 people. That took 20 years." He was then asked by the Minister of Petroleum to advance Saudi's mining sector and was given three key objectives: help create a new mining law that would be attractive to international companies; reorganise the bureaucracy and running of the Ministry of Oil & Minerals; and set up Ma'aden as a joint stock company that would eventually be listed.

The economic arguments for developing its mining presence are huge. Dabbagh says: "Saudi Arabia is two million square kilometres and has more than 100 locations for gold. We have done very little exploration in the past and there is now an opportunity to create the jobs that will utilise a large amount of manpower."

BLENDING POLITICS WITH COMMERCE: A JEDDAH PERSPECTIVE

Dabbagh is not alone. Another fascinating perspective comes from Abdullah Mouallimi, who spent four years as mayor of Jeddah, from 2001-2005. Today he runs DAR Consulting, a specialist company that provides advice to family firms on how to develop their domestic and international businesses. He says: "The Kingdom is not just about what happens in Riyadh. We are working very hard to position ourselves as the commercial centre for the country and ultimately the region. This is a realistic ambition."

International companies can now open certain types of businesses in the region and maintain 100 per cent stakes. The new Foreign Investment Law provides market access with a shortened black list of sectors, which must stay resolutely Saudi – for instance, the retail sector – but by and large there is a movement to welcome international business. The efforts that have been made to protect copyright are also seen as an example of best practice in the region.

Secondly, WTO membership means that foreign banks are able to open branches and launch joint venture agreements with local providers. The first example of this was BNP Paribas of France which opened a branch in Riyadh within days of WTO membership being sealed. It will be the first of many.

All of these trends are part of a plan by the government to wean itself off a dependency on "black gold". According to *The Economist*[5], non oil-forecasts were predicted to reach $17.5 billion in 2005, an increase of ten per cent on the previous year.

It is this practical outlook that won the acclaim of the World Bank. And it is a truism that the rest of the Arab world looks up to Saudi Arabia for direction on developing international businesses of repute. Each September, *Gulf Business* magazine produces its list of the 150 largest companies. The latest review in September 2005 included 11 Saudi companies out of the top 15.

Names such as **SABIC**, Saudi Telecom Company, Al Rajhi Banking and Investment and Riyadh Bank dominate the skyline of the Saudi economy. The constituents of the booming Saudi stock market invariably include the ruling Al Saud family on their shareholder register. These businesses are increasingly being run along the lines of leading international ones and are examining which best practice operations to develop.

For instance **SABIC**, the petrochemicals and steel group, is the largest industrialised business in the Middle East and one of the largest companies in the world. Today, its value is in excess of $150 billion, recognition that it is able to generate nearly $5 billion of profits on an annualised basis. The business, which is 70 per cent owned by the Saudi government and 30 per cent controlled by the private sector, will celebrate its thirtieth anniversary this year. It is companies such as these that are making ambitious bankers see the potential for international acquisitions of Western businesses, which could cement relationships and pace of growth.

Currently, there are just 76 companies listed on the Saudi stock market. Some, like Prince Fahad, hope to see that number increase to 250 over the coming years, but there is only so much capacity and capability to make the leaps forward that Saudi Arabia seems destined to fulfil.

REGIONAL PERSPECTIVE ON EGYPT

If it is reform for employment that is the chief driver and challenge for capital creation in the region today, the same siren call applies to Cairo as to Jeddah.

Outside Saudi Arabia, the push for political and economic reform continues. Egypt, for instance, arguably the second most important nation in the region after Saudi Arabia, has made some notable advances on the economic front, although its reputation for bureaucracy remains great. A new, economically liberal Cabinet was appointed in mid-2004, including five members of the Egyptian Competitiveness Council, a forward-looking think-tank. The cabinet has embarked on a programme of vigorous reform, slashing customs duties, loosening controls on imports and exports and announcing plans for sharp reductions in income tax and corporate tax rates. Crucially, President Mubarak has identified himself closely with the reform agenda.

5   A Long Walk – A survey of Saudi Arabia, January 7, 2006

The medicine appears to be working. Egypt is the most populous Arab country with nearly 70 million people, but is enjoying a period of economic strength. Boosted by gas exports, Suez Canal tolls and tourism revenues, there is every chance that its economic development will be a strong counterweight to any potential social problems.

But there are some big challenges ahead if it is to sustain its position, including the introduction of a privatisation programme and the lowering of widespread subsidies. These may prove a sterner test of Mubarak's resolve, but if they are waved through, they should help to improve Egypt's economic welfare.

A personification of these challenges can be found in Rachid Mohammed Rachid, the Egyptian Minister for Trade & Finance. The former Unilever man in the Middle East, with responsibility also for Africa and Asia as well as its global beverage business including Lipton Iced Tea, has never had to work so hard in his life. Sworn in on July 14, 2004, he resigned from the boards of 26 companies to commit his time and energy to boosting the Egyptian economy.

Like so many other businessmen turned politicians, he was attracted to the challenge of contributing to the development of his country. He was in Paris, visiting his daughter, when the telephone went and he was made the offer. He says: "I was told that I had 24 hours to decide. That is what keeps me up at night. Can I change the course of this country?"

His principal concern at the time was whether he would be given the chance to actually do what was needed to redevelop the economy successfully. "President Mubarak wants change, but in fact it is about the management of change, not the intention of change. I took the job in the hope that I can do something to assist," he says.

Like so many of his peers across the region, his principal objective is the creation of employment opportunities and wealth for his fellow Egyptians. He has officially 3.5 million unemployed people to deal with, but it is difficult to know the exact numbers. The focus is on doing things that will have a sustainable benefit. He continues: "This comes down to: (a) A disciplined development of a market economy in Egypt; (b) Integrate Egypt within the global economy; (c) Develop a true partnership with the private sector."

The indicators would seem to be going in the right direction. During the past 18 months, GDP has risen from three per cent to five per cent, inflation has fallen from 13 per cent to four per cent, FDI has grown from $1.9 billion to $3.9 billion, exports have increased by 30 per cent and the Egyptian stock market is one of the strongest in the world.

Question marks remain over the long-term viability of the Egyptian government to deliver and attract the necessary talent. He says: "The morale is actually very high. We have a number of exceptionally high-quality people in their twenties and thirties who have joined the government's bid to change things. They are coming from great jobs at P&G, Coke and Pepsi and believe that the change is for real and want to be part of it. They are a strong and very important constituency of believers and it is encouraging. The level of competencies and skills in the government had been faltering for 50 years. I have managed change programmes in businesses for many years. It is like any other management skills programme."

The comparison with business continues as he explains that the mantra for change is to communicate, over-communicate and then communicate again. "We have created what I call 'a burning platform'. Change is something that people do not generally like. If you make them realise that they are on a burning platform, they must jump into the sea. They must realise how bad things are before they are willing to accept change."

Those who have managed to swim ashore from the burning platform can see further benefits. The new trade agreements that have been completed and implemented with the European Union are good. The country is now moving on to stage two, including the launch of qualified industrial zones with the United States and Israel, which is in effect the creation of 450 export opportunities for Egyptian companies that are willing to make use of parts that come from Israel. These companies have special tax status when they export to the US and it makes a material difference. Finally, there is the creation of the Arab Free Trade Agreement that has incorporated 11 countries. It will be a precursor to an Arab Economic Market. A group of like-minded reformers in the region are going to drive change.

Rachid believes he is creating a tipping point and economics will be pulling past politics over the coming times. "We had it the other way round and it does not work. We can create a new reality for people and we have wasted enough time doing it the other way."

The Egyptian equities markets have responded very positively to the reformist developments within Egypt. In 2003, it was the seventh best performing stock market in the Morgan Stanley Capital International's index of emerging markets. In 2004 it was second and in 2005 it came first.

Will this momentum be sustained? In classic emerging market terms, the exchange is weighted exceptionally heavily towards the performance of its largest constituents, Orascom Telecom and Orascom Construction Industries. The market now requires the next generation of privatisations to be launched, which will have a material impact on the development of the region.

THE UAE REAL ESTATE BOOM

Dubai has become the crane capital of the world's construction industry.

It is just one of seven Emirates but has the largest non-oil-led plan. Much of this diversification rests on a real estate strategy that is huge in its expectation.

A recent report in *Arabian Business* magazine[6] listed the large-scale, long-term projects that are

6   *Arabian Business* magazine, January 29, 2006

re-shaping the skyline. Names such as "The Palm", "The World", "The Lost City" and "Dubailand" are moving from architects' drawings into reality. Each brick, stone and piece of concrete solidifies an ambition to become the Singapore of the Middle East, with excellent infrastructure to deliver it. Consequently economic free zones – Dubai Media City and Dubai Internet City – have emerged as sprawling hubs to become Middle Eastern versions of Silicon Valley.

In classic Hollywood parlance, if you build it, he will come. The risk appears to be paying off. The UAE is becoming regional home to a number of multinational organisations, such as Nokia. The arrival of multinationals triggers a need for homes and leisure facilities, not all of which are as outlandish as the world's largest indoor ski resort, which recently opened in Dubai.

But who is investing in all of these initiatives? The reality is that the government remains the biggest sponsor or benefactor of the real estate boom. The UAE's two largest real estate developers, Emaar Properties and Al Nakheel Properties, were both launched by the Dubai government. Emaar remains a third owned by the government. The government's corporate office continues to own the latter. This raises a number of issues. Eventually governments need to decide if they are regulators or owners. One sceptic of the UAE government says: "Every question you ask, they think like a real estate owner. Dubai is a real estate play and that philosophy comes from the top down."

Both Emaar and Al Nakheel are creating the most extravagant new developments. These are as much about promoting Dubai internationally as they are about fundamentally developing new flats. For instance The Palm Islands, an Al Nakheel project, consists of three tree-shaped archipelagos which are totally man-made.

The demand from other institutions both in the region and internationally is growing, following a decision in May 2002 when Sheikh Mohammed bin Rashid Al Maktoum issued a decree allowing foreigners to buy property in selected areas of the city on a freehold basis. Consequently, by early 2004, residential property prices were growing at an annual rate of ten per cent with villas increasing in 2005 by more than 20 per cent.

This is what has prompted the huge rush to develop new projects. Andy McTiernan is editor of *Dubai Property* magazine and was recently quoted as saying: "Originally people were speculating. You saw Saudis buying 40 apartments one day, and flipping them the next for a premium of up to 30 per cent. The speculation era petered out in early 2005 once lots of new projects became a reality."

Developers such as Emaar will in decades to come be viewed as brilliant futurists who turned the desert into a global hub, spoken of in the same breath as New York, London and Shanghai. Or they will be ridiculed for the empty follies that stand tall and empty. It is difficult to obtain accurate figures as to the scale of development within the region but it certainly runs into the tens of billions of dollars and may well be nudging past the hundreds.

Take Dubailand for instance, being constructed by Dubai Holdings, which is destined to complete in 2008. It is a $5 billion attempt to generate a Middle Eastern version of Disneyland. It is actually composed of 45 separate projects that will range from a space exploration exhibition to a full-size dinosaur enclosure. Including the Mall of Arabia, several new five-star hotels with one built out of sand dunes, and an indoor ski slope, it will also incorporate the largest zoo in the Middle East.

Of course there is much more to the UAE than just property in Dubai. There is no quicker way to insult someone from Abu Dhabi than to focus just on its smaller sibling; albeit one that uses incredible nous to market itself effectively.

Dubai polarises opinion. Some view it as akin to a regional freak show, a land built on steroids and growing at a pace that is filled with limited style and even less substance. Others congratulate it for having the strength to determine a vision that was not reliant on oil, and going after it; for changing the perception of the Arab world and becoming the Spain of the Middle East to Anglo-Saxon tourists.

On a commercial level it is undoubtedly a bricks and mortar play rather than a share certificate one. However frothy the markets get in the region – and at the time of writing they have just endured a mini correction – the focus for property at an institutional and retail level is incredible. This is a surge to put Dubai in the same league as Singapore. However, cynics complain that it is much closer to resembling Bangkok, which also has appalling traffic problems and daily issues of gridlock.

Visit Abu Dhabi though and you get the sense of a sleepy giant beginning to flex its considerable muscle. Like Dubai, construction is everywhere, but scratch the surface and there is a real resolve to branch into industrial complexes, infrastructure and cluster communities. With enormous reserves of cash spawned by the recent oil surpluses (Abu Dhabi Investment Authority is one of the most important global investor organizations) and a young generation of business savvy technocrats in charge, the next few years are going to be very much about the acceleration of growth in Abu Dhabi.

NATURAL GAS GLORY IN QATAR

Saudi Arabia and the UAE may capture much of the international coverage, but Qatar is increasingly emerging as one of the most important strategic places on earth. It is blessed with meaningful amounts of oil and is a member of OPEC, without figuring in its list of leading producers. However, it has the world's third largest reserves of natural gas and is set globally to become the richest state in per capita terms.

First-time visitors to Doha, capital of the state, see a rapidly changing skyline and often compare it with Dubai. This is a mistake as the changes in Qatar go much deeper than mere buildings suggest.

Western business partners often say that Qatar represents an optimistic future for both modernisers and traditionalists. After gaining independence from the UK in 1971, it remained a Gulf backwater until 1995 when Crown Prince Hamad bin Khalifa deposed his father to become Emir. His first 11 years in control have seen a dramatic improvement in the lives of the 200,000 Qatari citizens, who represent about a quarter of the people, living in the nation.

The chief highlights have been granting women the right to vote and stand for office in the municipal council elections, launching the Al-Jazeera satellite television service and drafting a Constitution which was launched in 2005. Qatar's proven gas reserves – thought to account for at least 15 per cent of what exists – will turn it into one of the most powerful energy nations over the next decade.

Bernard Picci is an energy analyst at Foresight Research. He recently wrote a report predicting that gas will replace oil as the world's key energy this century. It stated: "Qatar is Exhibit A in one of the most profound shifts in the history of world energy: the change from an oil-dominated energy complex to an increasingly gas-ruled energy world."

Jake Ulrich is head of international development at Centrica, owner of British Gas, in the UK. He spends the majority of his time on a plane racing from one potential new source to another and is exceptionally excited by the future strength of Qatar. He says: "Take the UK for instance. It is transitioning from being self-sufficient for its gas to becoming a net importer. The need to source and guarantee new supplies is a chief challenge facing the country and we are going to be increasingly looking to nations such as Qatar to support our requirements."

He is not alone. Shell had until 2003 one employee in the country. Today it is, according to the Financial Times, set to start work on a new $10 billion investment programme in the Emirate. Andrew Brown, who is the newly appointed head of its operations in the region, says that Qatar is quite simply "the most exciting place in the energy field in the world".

Given that the International Energy Agency believes world demand for gas will double by 2030, Qatar is exceptionally well placed to accelerate its position in the region.

Meanwhile it is expected to hold elections to a new parliament by early 2007. The Economist Intelligence Unit has forecast that GDP will expand by 9.3 per cent in 2006 and 8.3 per cent in 2007, enjoying a huge surplus that will continue to fund a generous series of state benefits for its already rich people. For instance, its education system now includes a series of US university branches and specialised teaching hospitals are being imported into a country where 60 per cent of the population is under 21. These include the Carnegie Mellon University of Pittsburgh, Pennsylvania, a member of Education City, which is focused on improving the calibre of human capital in future Qatari generations.

This population is excited and enthusiastic about its financial future. One only needs to look at the performance of the 33 stocks traded on the Doha Stock Exchange to see how excitable they are, and the government has liberalised the markets to allow non-Qataris to invest as well. When the Qatar Gas Transportation Company was listed in April 2005, the demand was obscene. According to a report in the *Financial Times*, people became so desperate that the identities of 131 dead people were used to apply for stock. Even worse, a group of 72 people applied for shares under a total of 3,152 names, leading to huge question marks over the handling of the issue. Even so, shares with a face value of Qr10 finished the first day of trading at Qr71 and are today Qr34, giving it a market capitalisation of $5.4 billion.

THE WIDER REGION

Space precludes a detailed overview of the wider Gulf and Levant region. Each market is distinctive in its own right and undergoing a similarly dramatic rate of growth. It is interesting to hear voices from different regions describe the variations of what is happening.

For instance Bahrain, an oil-rich Gulf state, is as eager to develop a regional hub for commerce as Qatar and the UAE. It remains too reliant on oil to stand much of a chance; however, it is developing an environment that is receiving lots of commendation. For instance the American Heritage Foundation, a think-tank, and *Wall Street Journal* combine each year to produce an index of Economic Freedom. It measures 161 countries against a list of 50 independent variables divided into ten broad factors of economic region. In the 2005 edition Bahrain came 20th out of 161 states and was the freest Arab economy.

The report said: "Bahrain is one of the most advanced economies in the Persian Gulf. Bahrain maintains a pro-business environment with low inflation, an excellent banking and finance system, strong property rights, low regulation and low barriers to foreign investment"

Oman is another member of the Gulf facing a fascinating future. Its Western borders are with the UAE, Saudi Arabia and the Yemen and is a country focused on defining its own unique approach to the world. Samir Fancy is the chairman of Renaissance Services, Topaz Energy and Marine and Tawoos, and is seen as one of the leading figures in the Omani business community. He is based in Muscat and oversees one of the fastest growing oil services groups in the region.

He says: "Unlike most other lower Gulf States, 80% of Oman's population is local and the interesting dynamic is that 60% of this number is under 19 years of age. This makes for a really dynamic environment with serious challenges and great long-term opportunity on which the government is resolutely focused."

Oman's family controlled companies are experiencing the same issues and asking the same questions as others in the region. Fancy says: "In 1997 during the first stock market boom the family company Tawoos decided to go into the oil and gas services industry. We spearheaded an initiative to acquire and simultaneously IPO a privately held company based in Dubai. The IPO was a huge success and we raised US$1.08 Billion against an offering of $22M. It was a sign of the times."

"Today Renaissance our public arm is amongst the top 5 listed corporations in the country. In 2005 it decided to enter the Oil and Gas services business. It acquired Topaz in an all paper offer in excess of $100M and then acquired Bue Marine at an enterprise value of around $120M. The resulting merger of the shipping fleets of the two companies created the 9th largest fleet servicing offshore installations in the world. This became the fifth major service business in Renaissance's portfolio. The move which was strategic in its intent and timely in its execution has been great for the group and growth has been exponential thus far".

In terms of what this means for the role of capital markets and private equity, he says: " The failure of Arab business to grow and cross borders is largely due to their inability to delegate and an obsession with control. When we floated Renaissance in 1996 so many families from Oman and the wider region spoke to us about our experiences. But ultimately few followed. Today as globalisation kicks in and scale starts to matter a realisation is setting in that families cannot afford to stay within their self imposed insular borders. Many of these companies will come to the market and private equity firms will be phenomenally positioned to take advantage of deal flow. The private equity firms will bring value, cross border transactions and efficiencies. At a time when the public equity market is fully priced to say the least, the real value will be in quality private equity."

There are individual books to be written on the wider region. Countries in the Levant such as Jordan, Lebanon and one day Palestine will all warrant the individual attention that this book is here giving to the wider region. (It would be 1,000 pages in length if it attempted to be comprehensive in its first edition.)

An interesting perspective is whether Saudi Arabia, Egypt, the UAE and Qatar will continue to be the four engine economies of the region in times to come. For instance Iran, Iraq and Kuwait have the second, third and fourth largest proven oil reserves in the world today. Taken together they have more oil than Saudi Arabia, and may begin to challenge and change the perception of the region over the coming decades.

STOCKMARKETS: A PREREQUISITE FOR PRIVATE EQUITY

Critics often accuse journalism of writing the first draft of history without having any real sense of what the future may hold. Until spring 2006 the region's equity markets seemed to be on an inexorable journey up. The logic was simple. Huge oil surpluses, capital that was tired of dealing with Western markets and liberalising markets meant only one thing: greater stability and greater strength in the local markets. Then the correction came knocking a dent into the confidence of the region's equity strategists.

Tarek Fadlallah, an economist at Nomura International, wrote: "The Tadawul All Share Index has until recently continued setting new highs in gravity defying leaps that confused and concerned many analysts." He went on to write extensively about the role that behavioural finance – also known as investor psychology – plays in these markets.

It was John Maynard Keynes who wrote that "markets can stay irrational longer than you can stay solvent". The newspapers and magazines of the region are filled with worried letters from wives who ask for advice on persuading their husbands not to give up a good job to play the markets. The same letters were written in Amsterdam before the tulips frenzy and in London at the height of the dotcom craziness.

It would be easy to dwell on what has been a stock market bubble in some parts of the region. However, there are more important underlying trends to consider. For instance, liquidity from markets provides a potential exit route for governments seeking to privatise, families looking to transition their businesses and private equity owners looking to sell. Stock markets act as a lubricant to the international and domestic financial centres. They are incredibly important venues where investors and traders meet. Consequently, although the recent bubble in some markets has captured headlines, of greater importance is the growing strength that these markets are building.

Investcom, the EMEA mobile telecommunications service provider, has an integral role within the world's telecommunications industry, but locally its founders have a visceral connection with the city in which the company has its headquarters: Beirut.

The journey to Investcom's headquarters in downtown Beirut is fraught. Cars jostle for position on the busy roads, which are still in a state of disrepair long after the bitterly fought civil war. Taha Mikati, who set up the company back in 1979, was swiftly joined by his brother Najib. Both men are experienced industrialists and Najib served as Prime Minister of Lebanon until May 2005. They now hold the posts of chairman and deputy chairman respectively, but it is Taha's son, Azmi, who has become a symbol for the region's rapidly developing equity markets.

Azmi Mikati represents a new breed of Arab business leader. The dynamic chief executive of Investcom was educated at Columbia University in the United States, and was one of the youngest ever chief executives of a major regional business when he was appointed in 1998.

The business has keen ambitions to grow on an international basis and decided that the benefits of being a listed entity – access to stock market paper to fund acquisitions, a device to incentivise staff and a tool to raise a company's profile – far outweigh the increased scrutiny and coverage which goes with being listed.

Mikati's decision to list the group's shares on the Dubai International Financial Exchange (DIFX) has ensured his place in the local history books. Investcom was the first company to take this step on October 15, 2005, just weeks after the DIFX opened for business. It also raised funds from a Global Depository Share Offer in London for $741 million, a move that will almost certainly be followed by a number of other Middle Eastern companies.

He says: "Listing is a historic decision for any business. Ours has a vision of being a regional leader. We are striving to create something and feel that being a listed entity, both locally and internationally in London, can only be a positive."

There are, in fact, dozens of reasons why businesses choose to list and as the first decade of the 21st century unfolds, there are high hopes amongst managers and investors alike that Investcom's decision will be followed by many others. There is a palpable feeling of excitement in the Gulf and the Levant that this is a region whose capital markets are on the cusp of something new, something almost transformational.

"The region has a sense of hope at the moment. Politics will always play a key role but people want the opportunity to create wealth and build their lives. Economics is becoming ever more important," says Mikati.

Enthusiasm for the Gulf has fuelled a dramatic explosion in the value of its stock markets, and this should kindle the regional private equity market. A dynamic – albeit fledgling – stock market is a prerequisite for developing venture capital markets. Those who invest in private companies need to have a degree of certainty in the local and regional stock markets, since this is one of the principal ways in which they exit their investments.

Across the Middle East, there are 12 recognised exchanges. The largest is the Saudi Arabian exchange, which dominates the region, accounting for more than half the total value of all listed stocks. The Kuwait Stock Exchange is the second biggest in value terms; but the Abu Dhabi Stock Market and DIFX are expected to play an increasingly significant role.

There are a number of Gulf-wide economic initiatives that could have a major impact on the development of its capital markets. For instance, in 2010 there is meant to be a single currency launched for the six members of the GCC, which could lead to consolidation of its capital markets.

Exchange	Country	Market Capitalisation ($)	Example Stocks
Saudi SE	Saudi Arabia	$678.7bn	SABIC, Saudi Telecom
Kuwait SE	Kuwait	$120.13bn	NBK, PWC Logistics
Abu Dhabi SM	UAE	$105.89bn	Nat. Bank of Abu Dhabi
Dubai FM	UAE	$89.31bn	Emaar Prop.
CASE SE	Egypt	$73.27bn	Arab Cotton
Doha SM	Qatar	$70.62bn	Industries Qatar, QNB
Casa	Morocco	$63.24bn	Maroc Telecom
Amman SE	Jordan	$34.01bn	Jordan Dairy
Bahrain SE	Bahrain	$17.7bn	Investcorp, Batelco
Muscat SM	Oman	$12.56bn	Omantel, BankMuscat
BLOM	Lebanon	$9.2bn	Blom Bank
Tunis	Tunisia	$3.29bn	Tunisair

Figures correct as of April 2, 2006

INVESTOR TOURISM: SPOILT FOR CHOICE?

The level of interest in the region from investors is truly staggering. When Dana Gas decided to float on the Abu Dhabi Securities Market in 2005, it generated a new type of travel in the region, dubbed "investor tourism"[7]. Individuals and institutions across the region flew to Abu Dhabi in a desperate bid to obtain a slither of the $560 million of available shares. So high was the demand that analysts have suggested it was 200 times over-subscribed. This means that in excess of $100 billion was on offer from investors for Dana Gas.

Admittedly, the story is enticing. Dana Gas will be the region's first publicly traded private sector gas company and it has ambitious regional development plans. Yet the behaviour of many investors indicates not just a demand for good stories from the region, but also a dearth of supply.

The Dana Gas story is not alone. Qatar's Al Rayan Bank, Bahrain's Al Salam and the flotations of Tamweel and EITC in the UAE have all created new records in the face of seemingly insatiable levels of investor appetite.

It is not just new IPOs that have the potential to whet the appetite of investors. Follow-on fund-raisings are also having a huge impact. When Emaar of the UAE announced plans to raise fresh funds, its website nearly crashed, such was the demand from investors to back its plans.

[7]   Zawya.com: *Frenzy on the Floors, October 2005*

It is because of this lack of investment opportunities that the new exchange in Dubai is working round the clock to entice entrants to the market. Nasser Al Shaali, chief operating officer of the DIFX, says: "We expect activities to pick up as we add more members and this will gradually grow throughout 2006. We are trying to attract more companies, especially banks. We expect at least three IPOs to be added to the list by the end of this year [2005] and up to 10 IPOs in 2006."

The importance of this region's equity markets is critical to its development economically and politically. But healthy stock markets have a symbiotic relationship with private equity markets, and over the next decade, the companies that sit inside the portfolios of private equity firms are likely to drive the issuance of new stocks. Executives from within the private equity sphere and those from the great trading families of the region will be looking closely at the equity market as they ponder their next moves.

Many are expected to make a decision about whether to list in Saudi Arabia or the UAE over the coming years. Both options are seductive.

The Saudi Arabian exchange was the best performing stock market in the world during 2005. The country's Tadawul All Share Index currently has 776 constituents from within Saudi Arabia. It is by far the largest market in the region, accounting for more than half of all the aggregated market capitalisation of listed stocks across the 12 exchanges in the Middle East. Its performance during 2005 was extraordinary, rising by more than 70 per cent over the year. Daily volumes reached almost $2 billion and, according to analysts at HSBC, it has become the largest emerging market in the world.

The largest listed company in the entire region is Saudi Arabia's industrial giant, Saudi Arabian Basic Industries (SABIC). Number two is Saudi Telecom Company. In the Gulf, Emaar of Dubai is the leading listed property developer. Set up in 1997, its sales reached $1.43 billion in 2004. It launched 40 new real estate developments in that year alone, including the exclusive Burj Dubai, dubbed the tallest tower in the world.

Almost every week, another new statistic emerges to fuel the regional growth story. Companies are coming to market or thinking of it and those that do receive a rapturous response.

One of the reasons behind this unprecedented public market growth is related to the terrorist attacks that took place in New York on September 11, 2001. Since then, Middle Eastern investors have made a deliberate decision to invest their money locally, rather than internationally. Rising oil prices, low interest rates and a more liberal economic agenda are also playing a part and the collective result is that the stock markets of the Middle East are among the most energetic in the world.

Nonetheless, the number of listed stocks is minuscule when compared to the number of businesses in the region. Hundreds of assets remain locked inside the empires of the traditional trading families, who are just beginning to consider the opportunities afforded by a stock market exit.

Sheikh Sultan Bin Saqr Al Qassimi, the co-founder and managing director of GIBCA Group, is a leader of one of the region's most influential trading families. He sees the development of local stock markets as playing a key role in the liberalisation of the region. "Many families would not be comfortable selling businesses. They would not want to be seen to do so. But listing on the stock market has different connotations," he says. In other words, selling shares to investors is a much more acceptable – and respectable – alternative to a trade sale.

Azmi Mikati of Investcom may come from a culturally different background, but he also believes that stock markets have a role to play in the development of the Gulf and the Levant. "Being listed means there is greater scrutiny and means companies have to be more disciplined. Ultimately, this will generate better performance which can only be a good thing for the region," he says.

THE CONTRARIAN'S PERSPECTIVE: THE TRUE PRICE OF OIL

The wider region – be it the Levant or the GCC - brings echoes of what one sees and hears in Saudi Arabia, Egypt and the UAE. Whether one is confronted by the Starbucks culture that has permeated Kuwait or the hesitant steps forward being made in Jordan, the signal for economics to drive the region forward continues. However this marathon has only just begun.

Again, comparison with the booming economies of East Asia is illuminating. In the Arab world, the ratio of private to public investment hovers around 1.8 to 1, a level that has remained broadly unchanged since the start of the 1990s. This compares to a ratio of 5 to 1 in East Asia. Strip out its oil wealth and this remains an economic infant beside its ageing political sibling.

Break down the economy by sector and it pales in comparison to the East Asian story. The Arab manufacturing sector is small. Marble from Palestine and textiles from Morocco does not an economy make. Tourism – dependent on stability to truly grow – could be a huge secondary source of revenue in the region, particularly in the Levant, but images of unpredictable demonstrators do little to boost visitor numbers.

Laura Tyson, dean of London Business School, says what everyone knows, that free trade is the key: "Embedded in competitiveness is openness to trade. Over the past 25 years, countries that have embraced trade globalisation – that is, countries that have increased their exports as a proportion of GDP – have grown much faster than those that have not. If trade as a percentage of GDP rises, then long-term GDP growth rates are three per cent plus. If trade as a percentage of GDP falls, then GDP growth is lower than one per cent."

The Middle East scores poorly on both foreign direct investment and non-oil export measures. According to estimates from the World Bank, non-oil exports are around a third of the level they could be, given the region's natural endowments, size and geography.

Foreign direct investment, the World Bank believes, could be around five times higher than it is at present. No wonder Saudi princes are willing to talk freely about pending privatisations: they recognise that they are in a competitive market for international development.

There are, of course, many factors delaying the introduction of deep and widespread reform. Regional security issues and the risk of conflict are cited as reasons to justify the status quo. In reality, however, two other fundamental factors have played an equally important role.

The first is the rising price of oil. Taking Saudi Arabia as an example, net oil export revenues in 1972 were around $15 billion. By 1980, after the oil price hikes of the mid-1970s, this figure had soared to more than $200 billion. Over the following two decades, falling oil prices led to a drop in Saudi Arabian net oil export revenues to less than $50 billion by 1998.

However, this figure has doubled over the past six years, taking net oil export revenues to more than $100 billion. It is an experience that has been mirrored in every oil-exporting country of the Middle East and it has given many Arab leaders a sense of economic wealth and well-being, encouraging them to introduce limited reforms and postpone the widespread changes needed to usher in a period of sustained economic growth and job creation.

"I am worried about what a price of $65 a barrel for oil will do to slow down the pace of reform," says Professor Tarik Yousef, a specialist in Middle East economics at Georgetown University.

The longer-term issue is that the high oil price is almost certainly unsustainable. Behind it lies a demographic time bomb – enormous population growth and an excessive dependence on the public sector. Over the coming decades, economic and political change is imperative if real, sustainable growth is to be achieved.

Some economists argue that deep economic reform can only come about as a result of fundamental change, whether in the political leadership arena or from a dramatic economic crisis. In Latin America, for example, reforms were only undertaken when economic conditions had deteriorated to the point where there was a political imperative to change. While there are examples of more gradual reform and change, such as in China and Vietnam, it is clear that in the Arab world the availability of capital from rising oil revenues has reduced the pace of change, both economically and politically.

The reaction of the region to the falling oil price of the Eighties provides a perfect example of this process in action, in that it incited a significant programme of reform and economic improvement. In the mid- to late-1980s, a number of countries, led by Morocco, Tunisia, Jordan and Egypt, found themselves facing high debts, deteriorating budget deficits and a lack of growth. They adopted programmes aimed at restoring macroeconomic balance and promoting the private sector as an engine of growth. By the end of the decade, a number of forward-thinking policies had been adopted throughout the region.

On the face of it, these programmes have achieved a good deal of success. Large and unsustainable fiscal deficits have been reduced by about two-thirds, through debt renegotiation and write-offs. Total external debt across the region has fallen from an average of 40 per cent of gross national income in 1990 to 28 per cent in 2002. The countries that were quickest to move down the reform path, namely Morocco, Jordan, Yemen and Egypt, have achieved the best results. It appears that the improvements gained through these positive measures have been sustained.

However, while the region has made significant gains in attaining macroeconomic stability, there are underlying pressures that threaten and weaken the system. Implicit debt (that which is not immediately apparent on a country's national accounts) is being pushed on a number of fronts, from pension system liabilities and the banking sector to private enterprise and government guarantees.

Yet there remains resistance to further social, economic and political change, characterised by state planning, the protection of local markets, and a widespread and cherished view of the state as principal provider of welfare, social services and even employment. Economic policies have been characterised by protectionism, highly regulated labour markets and a desire to protect employment, regardless of the long-term implications. Even where the private sector has played a significant role, such as in infrastructure construction, it has done so with the patronage of governments. Serious questions are justifiably raised about the way such contracts are allocated, and corruption is a massive issue.

History has proved that private enterprise is a crucial driver of wealth creation. Almost every country that has experienced sustained periods of economic growth and development has adopted this credo, from Britain in the Victorian era to the United States in the 20th century. Conversely, economic depression is an engine for profound political change. The French Revolution, the Russian Revolution and the recently adopted open-door policy of China have in reality been driven less by ideological imperatives than economic ones.

As the American satirist PJ O'Rourke observed, when commenting on the collapse of the Eastern bloc and the discrediting of communist philosophy: "A huge totalitarian regime with all its tanks and guns, gulags and secret police, was brought to its knees because no one wants to wear Bulgarian shoes."

The statement may sound flippant, but the underlying argument is clear.

Many poorly performing and dictatorial regimes have been usurped as their populations have become aware of their relative poverty. In the 20th century, as information began to flow more freely, through increased travel and improvements in technology, people began to see that they were living in societies that were not, as their governments had repeatedly told them, better off than those that had adopted the model of liberal democracy. This was true of the fall of the Eastern bloc, where cheaper and easier access to printing technology allowed wide dissemination of uncensored information. The parallels with the political upheaval that followed the invention of the printing press seven centuries ago are clear.

Two technological developments during the 1990s have taken this free flow of information to previously unknown heights: satellite television and the internet. These media have (with the exception of China) proved all but impossible to control. Indeed, the role of the Qatar-sponsored television station Al-Jazeera in the Arab world should not be underestimated. It has helped to create an environment of dialogue that has urged the ruling classes to make a choice: relinquish some control and open up to economic and political reform or lose control altogether.

If the Arab region were to replicate the economic performance of the 1990s in the current decade, then unemployment rates would rise from the current levels of around 13 per cent to 25 per cent by 2013. This is a wholly credible prediction, given that the public sector, traditionally the driver of the economy, is unlikely to remain the leading source of job creation. Low public sector worker productivity means that any expansion in public sector employment will come at an increased cost to the public purse, which it quite simply cannot afford.

PRIVATE SECTOR: BARRIERS TO ENTRY

So why has the private sector failed to flourish in recent years? Much of it is down to weakness in the investment climate, which historically discouraged entrepreneurship and new business creation. Barriers to entry for private firms, both in terms of the time and cost of administrative approvals, do not help.

A lot of this comes down to money. For new firms in Arab countries to comply with regulations it costs, on average, 75 per cent of per capita gross national income, more than double the 34 per cent in Eastern Europe, and dwarfing the 16 per cent in East Asia and 14 per cent in Latin America. In OECD countries, it takes an average of one month to register a business; in the Arab world the average is 60 days, although this number is falling by the month.

Financing, too, is a severe problem, driven by the attitude of banks in the area and the lack of venture capital financing. The financial system is dominated by public sector banks, which favour state enterprises, larger industrial concerns and offshore enterprises. The costs and barriers for small businesses raising capital are staggeringly high. The minimum capital required to start a business in the Middle East and North Africa is an average 1,500 per cent of per capita GDP. The figure is almost three times as high as East Asia, which itself has a high score of 700 per cent of GDP per capital. By contrast, in OECD countries the figure is just 64 per cent. On top of that, availability of finance for small and medium-sized enterprises (SMEs) is almost non-existent. SMEs in the region rely almost entirely on owner equity and retained earnings to finance their operations. In no Arab country does the banking system provide more than 25 per cent of investment financing, compared to 36 per cent in India and 47 per cent in Thailand.[8]

HOPE: A PLENTIFUL COMMODITY

All is not doom and gloom: it goes without saying that there are renewed reasons for optimism. Hope is a vitally important commodity in the region, especially when 20 per cent of the Middle East's inhabitants live on less than $2 a day. Like many emerging markets, there is a huge chasm between rich and poor. Petro-billionaires can live only a few hundred miles away from swathes of people who struggle to exist below the poverty line.

That does not mean there is no belief in a better future. A ground-breaking report from London think-tank the Portland Trust[9], examined the economic impact of peace on Palestinians and Israelis and found that even in one of the most strife-torn areas of this region, hope persists, alongside a conviction that capital has a key role to play in the years ahead.

The report interviewed 60 business people living in the West Bank and Gaza and concluded that the private sector can play a pivotal part in generating growth, sustainable employment levels and better living standards. Entrepreneurs in the region have proved amazingly resilient and their stance is remarkably consistent: if the private sector is left alone to get on with the job of making money, it will.

In less war-torn parts, the private sector is making steady strides in this direction. Confidence in many areas is high at the moment and regional stock markets are performing well.

Many factors have contributed to the situation. The booming oil price plays a part, of course, but markets have been helped too, particularly in the Gulf, by a number of well-timed reforms. These have liberalised economies and encouraged privatisation of state assets in the region. Rising real estate markets have also helped to turn this area into one of the most exciting emerging markets in the world.

The picture for economic development in the Arab world over the next 20 years is undoubtedly bleak, if present conditions prevail. However, the need and the desire for change are becoming increasingly hard to resist. In recent times, the high oil price has served to prop up failing economies and give the impression – to both governments and the populace at large – that reforms are less urgently needed. But the oil price will not stay at $60 or more per barrel forever.

An understanding of what needs to be done and, crucially, how to do it, exists at the highest levels, in the worlds of both business and politics. Countries may not exactly be embracing democracy with open arms, but they are beginning to travel down a road leading to more transparent societies with a higher standard of governance. Across the region, countries are pursuing privatisation programmes that will accelerate over time.

"We are strong believers in the role of the private sector and are in the process of expanding the privatisation process to include airports, borders and the energy sector,"

---

9   *Beyond Conflict: The Economic Impact of Peach on Palestinians and Israelis*, Portland Trust, December 2004

Sharif Ali Zu'bi, Minister for Industry & Trade in Jordan told the World Economic Forum earlier this year. If the privatisation of state assets across Europe, most notably in Britain, is any guide, this will have a dramatic trickle-down effect: it will introduce competitiveness and openness into the way in which these huge companies interact with their suppliers.

Across the region, states such as the United Arab Emirates, Bahrain and Qatar are vying to set up and build effective financial centres. They are looking at the success of institutions elsewhere in the world, from the most developed economies to the recently energised countries of East Asia. Already, these states have made great leaps transforming their economic and regulatory structures, and have reaped the benefits of increasing gross domestic product, job creation and the vitality of a robust private sector.

Many factors are driving the confidence of the Gulf. It is blessed with deep resources of black gold and equally valuable reserves of natural gas. The demand of emerging markets like China and India for these resources is providing huge reserves of capital that is being invested locally and internationally. It has also given the region the opportunity to invest to diversify and develop tourist and commercial hubs.

This is in marked contrast to other parts of the Arab world, which remain some of the poorest areas on earth. The levels of poverty in the Gaza Strip for instance, with the world's highest rates of unemployment, deeply saddens many. The future here is bleak and based on a culture of dependency. The role that private enterprise can play is absolutely critical to develop both these types of markets.

There is a deep irony that this region, where some of the world's deepest pockets of wealth co-exist with high levels of poverty, now has the best performing stock markets in its midst.

In recent years, stock markets in countries such as Saudi Arabia and Kuwait have grown by more than 200 per cent per annum, driven by the repatriation of capital in the aftermath of September 11. This is unlikely to continue indefinitely but, while a correction may well take place, the markets will continue to develop and mature over the coming decade.

John Hobday, head of Citigate Dewe Rogerson, a specialist financial communications company with operations in the Gulf, says: "I remember being in London during the internet boom, which was crazy. But this is worse. I walked down the street recently and a car pulled up beside me, asking where the stock market was. It was filled with kids who didn't know much about business, wanting to buy shares, because they had heard it was a good thing."

A strong capital market can sometimes get over-excited, but it is a fundamental rock on which private enterprise rests for financial support. The development of private enterprise is strong within the region, which is also harnessing a number of lessons that have been accessed from more advanced financial markets.

Techniques that took decades to evolve elsewhere can be and are being imported into the Arab region. These include the application of rigorous due diligence, market analysis and active management strategies to enhance and create value. The scale of the region's challenges should not be underestimated, but if there is a will to move towards a private-sector-driven, transparent and fair economy, then substantial progress can be made. It is an opportunity that regional players need to grasp with both hands. As one senior investor says: "There is a lot of expectation on private equity to deliver. We are aware of it and can contribute, but will only ever be part of the solution."

CULTURALLY REDEFINING DEMOCRATISATION

In his 2005 State of the Union address, President George W. Bush pledged to "help others find their own voice, attain their own freedom and make their own way". He also said he would "support the growth of democratic movements and institutions in every nation and culture". Practically speaking, the spread of principles embedded in Western democracies would bring significant strategic benefits to the United States and the rest of the world. Theoretically, at least according to the neo-conservatives who find their inspiration in the democratic peace argument, the democratisation of the region could alleviate political tension, ease economic reforms and improve wealth distribution to raise the standards of living.

Bush's words appeared to represent a significant change in Washington's approach to the Middle East. In the past, the US disregarded the internal order of the region's states as long as they supported US policy. September 11 taught them the price of ignoring the underlying causes of the regional population's discontent.

The status quo is no longer an option and US international political analysts advance two distinct alternatives to the past 60 years of support to Middle East oppression: neo-conservatism and neo-liberalism. Both theories argue that the spread of democracy is the surest drive to peace, but they are divided on the means to reach democratisation. The neo-conservatives favour the use of coercive action whereas the neo-liberals believe democratic change can only come about by addressing the roots of indigenous disgruntlement and encouraging reform from within.

However, the American administration's commitment to promoting domestic changes through in-depth reforms can already be questioned. The financial help allocated to democratic initiatives in the region was significantly lower in 2005 than in 2004. The Middle East Partnership Initiative (MEPI), which is the White House's flagship initiative intended to encourage political freedom, saw its budget cut by $300 million in that period. The funding issue illustrates the fact that the debate in Washington is still ongoing as to what constitutes the best peaceful approach for foreign powers to foster democracy in sovereign states

Unilateral sanctions, such as those practised with Cuba, North Korea, Iran and Syria, are blatantly ineffective as they hardly affect the targeted states. Multilateral sanctions have shown their limits; and in the end those who suffer the most are civilians.

Another practical *démarche* has, however, borne fruit in countries such as Ukraine, South Africa and the Philippines: long-term investment in grass-roots democracy-building. This involves pushing mass education; actively encouraging free press and the spread of information through printed and screen media; supporting economic reforms; and investing in modern economic structures that will deliver higher living standards and a better social environment. In the Arab world, as in many emerging markets, economic and political spheres are closely linked and the prominence of the state makes it key to the reform process, whether encouraging or impeding change.

GOVERNMENT-GOVERNMENT PARTNERSHIPS: FINANCING ECONOMIC REFORM

The European Union and, more recently, the US, have developed programmes aimed at instigating reforms that would transform Arab society in the long term. These seem to offer a comprehensive solution by establishing a system of basic, bottom-up democratisation. Whether it is the US MEPI programme or the EU Mediterranean and Middle East Aid Programme, both set wide areas of action and ambitious goals, thus requiring large amounts of financial support.

The MEPI has four pillars, for instance: economic reform, political reform, education and female empowerment. In concrete terms, the economic initiatives financially supported by MEPI revolve around enhancing global competitiveness, fostering foreign direct investments and facilitating entrepreneurship. The MEPI's political agenda aims to strengthen the role of free media, promote increased transparency and better governance, and encourage more involvement from the civil society. MEPI education initiatives are to widen access to school, especially for girls, encourage the teaching of employable skills and reform the curricula accordingly. Finally, MEPI also intends to increase the participation of women in society by reducing cultural, legal, economic and political barriers to their empowerment – in effect, enabling them to contribute financially to their families and the greater economy.

MEPI may have flaws – the lack of focus is an obvious one - but it identifies key areas for change, sets an all-inclusive agenda for in-depth democratic reforms, and invites NGOs, the private sector and local governments to take part in the process. MEPI-backed programmes in 2005 have included helping Algeria with its WTO application; creating links between American and Yemenite Universities; setting up an entrepreneurship fund in Jordan; and the implementation of child education centres in many North Africa and Gulf states. These projects all deliver real improvements to the lives of Arab men, women and children.

In recent years, EU and, to a much larger extent, US initiatives, have increasingly shifted their resources from social and educative schemes to economic programmes. This reflects an increasing belief that economic reforms will promote political liberty and social change. But it also means these initiatives favour local government and local aid programmes.

NGOs rely heavily on their field officers to select and devise grass-roots projects, but the US and EU programmes have worked closely with local embassies and local governments to allocate their aid. One reason for that is that Arab states have long relied on state-owned companies to foster growth and provide employment, whereas the private sector is very much reliant on governmental contracts to stay afloat. Due to the prominence of the public sector, economic changes and dynamism will have to come through its modernisation. Consequently, and unarguably, political and economic reforms will have to come hand-in-hand. Bottom-up initiatives are doomed to fail without top-down reforms. Local NGOs and the private sector, whether foreign or domestic, are indispensable to the initiation and funding of grass-roots projects. However, only regime-led reforms will deliver significant and durable changes. Whether oil-rich or not, Arab governments are always welcoming of financial help, but their reform agenda does not necessarily accord with their providers' wish list.

In the Levant, particularly in Jordan and more extensively in Egypt, leaders try to maintain their positions whilst accommodating only partial reforms. The key question facing Arab governments today is how much power to relinquish, now, to avoid foreign military pressure and alleviate potential domestic pressures in years to come. For Western powers, the question is how much financial incentive to give to those governments that show signs of embracing a liberalising agenda.

Citizens in Washington and European capitals are also worried that a sudden liberalisation in voting systems will benefit the sects of violent "radical" Islamic groups. Over the past decade, due to non-existent or strictly monitored press freedom in Egypt and Jordan, for instance, liberalism and other political alternatives have had very little exposure and enjoy limited popular support. However, some Islamic associations, funded by oil-rich neighbours, have made significant inroads into these civil societies by fulfilling the basic health and education needs of the poorest members of society.

Except for Lebanon, which has always been an exception in the region due to its multicultural and multi-religious diversity and European ties, it may take some time for modern democratic values to become the real alternative to autocratic rule. At the moment, as in Algeria at the end of last century, Islamic politics – sometimes radicalism – is the most likely beneficiary of President Mubarak or King Abdullah redistributing their power more legitimately. This analysis has been an excuse for Western powers to support tyrannical regimes in the Middle East for years.

As mentioned above, September 11 made the West and the US realise that supporting dictatorship was short-sighted and dangerous: further democratisation became the key tenet of their regional policies. If Jordan and Egypt's old friendship with the US kept them off the hook for military action, Washington has recently shown growing impatience in the face of sluggish liberalisation. The current Iraq war has given a new depth to their rhetoric and the US is now explicitly demanding political and economic reforms. Washington cannot afford to be seen subsidising autocracies without promoting reforms that will benefit the local population.

To sum up, given the central role played by the public sector, the private sector's input is crucial but alone it will not achieve significant and durable changes. This requires regime-led reforms. Official Western analysts have drawn the same conclusion, hence the government-government cooperation of organisations such as **MEPI**. However, US and European governments are now linking the funding of such programmes not only to quicker reforms, but also to democratisation. These reforms should provide the basis for an enhanced and energised private sector.

Peter Brabeck-Letmathe, chief executive officer of Nestlé, the world's largest food company, says: "The changes in the region in the past couple of years have been strong. Democracy has been on the march, such as suffrage for women in Kuwait. It is a unique opportunity. The region has 290 million consumers who, over the next 20 years, will become 580 million people with the right to adequate nutrition. We cannot afford not to be involved. But even the most successful company cannot prosper if the economic conditions are not right. That the region gets just one per cent of foreign direct investment is a cause for alarm. This is a sign that it is not changing fast enough, at least not fast enough for many private investors."

COUNTRY BY COUNTRY
STOCK EXCHANGES
These exchanges have been listed in order of size – by cumulative market value - with the largest first.

Saudi Arabia:
Saudi Arabian Exchange
(www.tadawul.com)
Name of Stock Market: Tadawul Stock Market
Number of stocks listed: 79

Top 5 Stocks by Market Capitalisation: (US $)
Sabic-$152.5bn
Saudi Telecom $85.08bn
Al Rajhi Bank $84.22bn
Saudi Electricity $32.60bn
Samba Financial $30.11bn

UAE:
Abu Dhabi
ADSM (www.adsm.co.ae)
Name of Stock Market: Abu Dhabi Securities
Market (ADSM)
Number of stocks listed: 40

Top 5 Stocks by Market Capitalisation: (US $)
Etisalat - $25.69bn
National Bank of Abu Dhabi - $12.41bn
Abu Dhabi Commercial Bank - $10.24bn
First Gulf Bank - $6.07bn
Dana Gas $5.35bn

Dubai:
Dubai FM (www.dfm.co.ae)
Name of Stock Market: Dubai Financial Markets
Number of stocks listed: 28

Top 5 Stocks by Market Capitalisation: (US$)
Emaar Properties - $31.70bn
Dubai Islamic Bank -$12.12bn
Emirates Bank (EBI) - $9.11bn
Mashreqbank $7.07bn

National Bank of Dubai - $5.79bn

Kuwait:
Kuwait Stock Exchange
(www.kse.com.kw)
Name of Stock Market: Kuwait Stock Exchange
(KSE)
Number of stocks listed: 133
Top 5 Stocks by Market Capitalisation: (US $)
National Bank of Kuwait (NBK) - $13.75bn
Mobile Telecommunications Company -
$12.61bn
Kuwait Finance House (KFH) - $8.64bn
Public Warehousing Company (The) - $5.62bn
Commercial Bank of Kuwait - $4.76bn

Oman:
Oman Exchange
(www.msm.gov.om)
Name of Stock Market: Muscat Securities Market
Number of stocks listed: 127

Top 5 Stocks by Market Capitalisation: (US$)
Oman Telecommunications Company - $2.48bn
BankMuscat - $2.11bn
National Bank of Oman - $1.01bn
Oman International Bank - $721m
Oman Cement Company - $469m

Bahrain:
Bahrain Exchange
(www.bahrainstockexchange.com)
Name of Stock Market: Bahrain Stock Exchange
Number of stocks listed: 44

Top 5 Stocks by Market Capitalisation: ($US)
Bahrain Telecommunications Company - $2.91bn
Ahli United Bank (AUB) - $2.41bn
Gulf Finance House - $1.99bn
Investcorp Bank - $1.88bn
Arab Banking Corporation $1.20bn

Qatar:
Qatar Exchange
(www.dsm.com.qa)
Name of Stock Market: Doha Securities Market
- DSM
Number of stocks listed: 33

Top 5 Stocks by Market Capitalisation: (US$)
Industries Qatar - $16.58bn
Qatar National Bank - $8.39bn
Qatar Telecom - $6.51bn
Qatar Gas Transport Company - $6.14bn
Commercial Bank $5.47bn

Morocco:
Morocco Exchange
(www.casablanca-bourse.com)
Name of Stock Market: Bourse de Casablanca
Number of stocks listed: 59

Top 5 Stocks by Market Capitalisation: $US
Afriquia Gaz $29.46bn
Maroc Télécom - $13.90bn
Attijariwafa Bank - $3.99bn
Groupe ONA - $2.55bn
Lafarge Ciments - $2.03bn

Lebanon:
Beirut Stock Exchange
(www.bse.com.lb/)
Name of Stock Market: Beirut Stock Exchange
Number of stocks listed: 15

Top 5 Stocks by Market Capitalisation: ($US)
Solidere - $2.25bn
Banque Audi - $1.59bn
Blom Bank - $1.52bn
Byblos Bank- $1.17bn
Bank of Beirut - $639bn

Jordan:
Jordan Exchange
(www.exchange.jo)
Name of Stock Market: Amman Stock Exchange
Number of stocks listed: 177

Top 5 Stocks by Market Capitalisation: ($US)
Arab Bank - $14.41bn
The Housing Bank for Trade and Finance
-$2.92bn
Jordan Telecom - $1.90bn
Arab Potash Company (APC) - $1.39bn
Jordan Cement Factories Company - $1.24bn

Egypt:
Egypt Exchange
(www.egyptse.com)
Name of Stock Market: Cairo and Alexandria
Stock Exchange
Number of stocks listed: 331

Top 5 Stocks by Market Capitalisation: ($US)
Orascom Telecom Holding - $12.1bn
Orascom Construction Industries - $8.48bn
Telecom Egypt $4.86bn
Vodafone Egypt - $3.92bn
EFG Hermes Holding Company $3.79bn

Tunisia:
Tunisia Exchange
(www.bvmt.com.tn)
Name of Stock Market: Bourse Des Valeurs
Mobilières De Tunis (BVMT)
Number of stocks listed: 50

Top 5 Stocks by Market Capitalisation: ($US)
Banque de Tunisie - $445.2m
Société Frigorifique et Brasserie de Tunis
- $340.5m
Banque Internationale Arabe de Tunisie
- $354.9m
Union Bancaire pour le Commerce et l'Industrie
- $211.5m
Arab Tunisian Bank $151.4m

This information was correct as of Tuesday April 11th, 2006

Chapter 2

The surge of private equity

BOOM TIME IN PRIVATE EQUITY: A GLOBAL PERSPECTIVE

The development of the private equity industry from what was effectively a cottage industry as recently as the early 1980s into today's emperor of the capital markets remains one of the great business tales of the past century.

The emergence of an industry, truly global in outlook yet intensely local in practice, is changing the shape of the world's equity markets. The private equity industry has become home to some of the brightest financiers in the world and is leading to keen debates about the most effective structures for the management of companies.

It is an industry that has to become more attuned to public scrutiny despite its private ambitions. During 2005 it accounted for funds being raised of $261 billion[10], eclipsing the dotcom inspired peak of 2000 when $254 billion was raised. The industry fully expects 2006 to beat last year and some optimists believe it could breach $300 billion of funds being raised next year.

It is difficult to fully appreciate its significance, but worth trying. Investment banks understand it. According to research[11] that focused on the European market, they obtained fees in excess of E1.2 billion from servicing the needs of those funds. Business leaders realise. Jack Welch, the legendary ex-head of GE, is now at US buyout specialist Clayton, Dubilier & Rice. The political elite certainly get it. Carlyle, one of a handful of truly global operators, has a knack of putting senior politicians to work including George Bush senior and Fidel Ramos, the former President of the Philippines.

Where did it all begin? Who was the first venture capitalist, as people in the industry prefer to be known? David Rubinstein, one of the global leaders of the industry, who founded and leads Carlyle, often opens up his conference speech by explaining why the crown belongs to Christopher Columbus. "In 1492, he persuaded European investors to fund an international voyage of discovery and organised a well-structured rewards scheme dependent on the performance of the trip," says Rubinstein.

Columbus had built a strong track record as a navigator and sailor who undertook his first voyage at the tender age of 19. Then, he visited destinations as far-flung as Iceland and Guinea. His principal target remained the route to the Indies and the lucrative spice trade which he believed could be opened up, as a consequence of heading west from Europe. He approached King John of Portugal for funding for the venture, dubbed "The Enterprise of the Indies", in 1484, but was rebuffed.

Columbus moved to Spain and began lobbying King Ferdinand and Queen Isabella of Spain for the investment capital. In 1492, after six long years, the monarchs finally bought into the concept. They became investors in the project, giving Columbus three ships and a crew of 90

---

10   The 2006 Global Fund Raising Review, published by Private Equity Intelligence
11   Dealogic M&A fees from European Private Equity in 2005

men. Columbus' experience was by no means unique, either then or now. Any modern private equity practitioner who has attempted to set up a new fund will empathise with Columbus over the time taken to gain the support of his backers.

In fact, King Ferdinand and Queen Isabella could be described as the first limited partners. The term, widely used in today's financial markets, describes organisations which invest in private equity funds. The principals who raise the funds and then select which companies to invest in are known as general partners.

Although Columbus may have been disappointed to discover America – he had, after all, been hoping to find Asia and its cities made of gold – his investors were repaid many times over as the discovery and subsequent exploitation of that country laid the foundations for one of the most powerful empires Europe had ever seen.

One key difference, however, between Christopher Columbus and latter-day private equity practitioners is that most of them invest in mature businesses, rather than completely unknown enterprises. So the start-up expedition represented by Columbus, raising capital to back a venture into an emerging market, is a more appropriate symbol of private equity's more buccaneering cousin, the venture capital industry.

Nonetheless, the Columbus experience makes one point abundantly clear: transactions where private companies and individuals are funded in such a way as to help them and their investors are as old as business itself.

Goldman Sachs has conducted research and believes there are currently more than 2,700 private equity firms in the world.[12] Although the great majority are to be found in the developed world, an increasing number have been set up in emerging Asian, Middle Eastern and Latin American markets.

While the basic concept of private equity is clear – money is invested in businesses in such a way as to deliver above-average returns for shareholders – definitions can be stretched.

The Anglo-Saxon approach personified by the emergence of an ever-increasing number of funds managed by general partners with investor support from limited partners is often seen as the classical structure for private equity. But there are other types of structure focused on investing in and then improving the performance of private companies in a rapid period of time.

There are, for instance, a large number of individuals who raise funds on a deal by deal basis. They can be just as organised as any fund but prefer to work on that basis. Before launching into a detailed explanation of where private equity is today and how it is driving change in the Middle East, it makes sense to pause and examine its genesis.

The genesis and development of the industry

Christopher Welch, a director at Meketa Investment Group, which provides a range of private equity advisory services, argues that 1981 – rather than 1492 - marked the key turning point in the history of private equity. "That was when the State of Oregon committed $195 million to Kohlberg Kravis Roberts, becoming the first institutional investor to back a private equity fund," he says.

Even today, pension funds and endowments remain the single largest investor in the private equity asset class. But that investment by the State of Oregon can be seen as the first step in the transformation of the industry from a bit player into a distinctive asset class in its own right, helping to change the perception of private equity into something more than just an advanced form of corporate finance. Whether Oregon realised the role it was playing is unclear, but private equity practitioners the world over should congratulate the state for its foresight and progressiveness in backing the launch of a new industry.

Today there are thousands of private equity firms across the globe. Each has ambitions to develop a blue chip investor base and a track record of investing in companies that subsequently achieve an exceptional return, thanks to the way they are managed and developed under the stewardship of the private equity investor.

Of course, the industry was helped on its way by the support of pioneering investors such as the state of Oregon. But it was also given a massive boost by the development of the debt markets through the 1980s.

Smart financiers such as Henry Kravis, co-founder of Kohlberg Kravis Roberts, were able to launch their businesses by the clever use of debt. In fact, they were utterly reliant on leverage. The maths is simple. If a private equity operator bought a company for €200 million and used €20 million of its own equity to fund the deal, it needed €180 million of debt. If it subsequently sold the business for €220 million, it doubled its money. After paying down the €180 million of debt, it was left with €40 million compared to its original stake of €20 million.

During those early years, private equity focused primarily on the efficient use of leverage. The key pioneers during the 1980s were financial engineers, but today there are a myriad of strategies which are applied as firms pit their wits against the markets and each other in a bid to deliver robust returns to themselves and their investors.

Simply put, these strategies can be boiled down to improving the profitability of acquired companies; the judicious selection of undervalued companies; and a willingness to consider breaking up companies that need to be transformed.

The reality is that the industry did not really begin in 1492 or 1981: there are a number of other key milestones that any student of the subject needs to be aware of. Many of the sector's origins are to be found in the United States. During the 1920s affluent US families began to supply start-up capital for new ventures. They believed that spreading their risk into early-stage and private companies was a sensible diversification strategy, given that the majority of their assets were invested in public stocks and property.

This is in fact no different from the actions of many ruling and trading families in the Middle East today. They are following in the footsteps of their US counterparts by investing to diversify.

Today these families would be called business angels. Indeed, there are clusters of networks throughout the world in which wealthy benefactors provide capital and experience to assist early-stage companies. The size of this informal investment market is difficult to gauge, though it is undoubtedly significant. Professor Colin Mason of Strathclyde University, an expert on the phenomenon, estimates that UK business angels make between 3,000 and 6,000 investments a year, possibly totalling £1 billion.[13] Meanwhile, according to the website of the University of New Hampshire's Centre for Venture Research, US business angels now invest a total of $40 billion in around 50,000 deals a year.

Back in the 1920s, these angels or benefactors operated on an informal basis. But, following the Wall Street crash in 1929 and the subsequent economic depression in the US and Europe, governments in the UK and America set about examining new initiatives to stimulate the economy. In 1931, the Macmillan Committee was created in the UK to investigate the economic malaise that had gripped the country. It identified what it described as an "equity gap" and concluded that the government had to make it easier for small and medium-sized businesses to gain access to capital. Some years later, the UK government acted on this advice. In the immediate aftermath of World War II, it set up two organisations to help rebuild the crippled country: Finance and Capital for Industry (FCI) was formed to supply larger amounts of capital to bigger businesses and the Industrial & Commercial Finance Corporation (ICFC) was created for smaller companies.

The institutions were financed with capital provided by the UK's largest banks. The ICFC was the forerunner of today's 3i, which is now a FTSE 100 company in the UK. 3i has more than 250 investment professionals working from 28 local offices in 13 countries, investing right across the globe in a range of private businesses.

3i has come into its own in recent years. But it was in the post-World War II environment of the United States that the private equity industry really began to emerge. The US government recognised the need to reinvest in the infrastructure of America and in 1946 it created American Research & Development (ARD). The organisation was charged with helping small private companies to fulfil their ambitions by supplying them with the development capital they needed. Early investors included the John Hancock Life Assurance company.

Many companies wanted to obtain capital without ceding all their equity, which led to the creation

---

13   *Barriers to growth in UK small businesses*, a research report by Professor Colin Mason of the Hunter Centre of Entrepreneurship at the University of Strathclyde

of regulated Small Business Investment Companies (SBICs) in the 1950s. The difference between these and the approach of ARD was that capital provided by the SBICs was in the form of debt. The approach proved successful and more than 500 companies were formed under the scheme during the late 1950s. New investor firms were set up to specialise in the running of these investments and they became the forerunners of today's private equity funds.

The industry continued to grow slowly but developed at a much faster pace following a series of legislative changes implemented to counter the weak economic markets of the 1970s. One of the most significant US government initiatives was the 1978 Revenue Act, which reduced capital gains tax from 50 per cent to 28 per cent. The capital gains tax rate was then cut further to 20 per cent in 1981. This provided a significant boost to equity investment and, interestingly, actually led to an increase in the total amount of revenue generated by capital gains tax, despite the lower rate.

Between 1979 and 1989, the number of companies in the US attracting funding rose more than fourfold to 1,700 per annum.[14] As the market developed, so too did the investor base, moving away from its reliance on wealthy private individuals and university endowment funds to bring in pension funds, banks and other institutional investors.

Meanwhile, in the UK, the industry began to grow beyond the confines of 3i, which for a time was synonymous with venture capital in the country. High-street banks, including National Westminster, Barclays and Lloyds, began to establish their own private equity units. The British Venture Capital Association saw its membership grow from 30 in 1980 to more than 120 by 1990. This growth was assisted by the appearance of a new exit market, the Unlisted Securities Market (USM), which was created by the London Stock Exchange in 1982 as an avenue for smaller companies.

For there is a direct correlation between the buoyancy of public markets and the ability of private equity funds to achieve the exits they need and want. When public markets are riding high, there are clear windows of opportunity, allowing investments to be exited or sold at high valuations.

This basic fact operates on a global basis. It is equally applicable to emerging markets such as Eastern Europe or the Middle East. Exits are achieved either by the sale of shares on the public market through an initial public offering (IPO) or, more commonly, through trade sales, when a private equity investment is sold to an existing business.

In general, companies are more acquisitive when stock markets are rising, partly because they can raise the funds cheaply to pay for their acquisitions and partly because they can use their own shares as acquisition currency. These profitable exits fuel the cycle of private equity, returning funds back to investors, and enabling the partners to go out and raise fresh funds.

14   *The Kings of Capitalism*, Peter Temple

MARKET SEGMENTATION

As the private equity industry has developed, it has undergone a degree of segmentation common to all evolving financial markets. Private equity funds have become classified according to the type of investments that they make. At one end are the huge funds completing billion-dollar deals, which are sometimes described as mega-funds.

This is the glamorous end of the market and attracts most of the attention of the media. Take, for example, Kohlberg Kravis Roberts's $29 billion acquisition of RJR Nabisco in 1989, which was first turned into a best-selling book, *Barbarians at the Gate*, before being made into a Hollywood film. Much of the return in such an instance is generated through the application of innovative and clever financing techniques, including securitisation and high yield bonds, which work because the companies being bought tend to be market leaders with stable and predictable earnings.

Below this level come the mid-market investors. They are focused on investing smaller amounts in mid-sized companies. They may not attract the same amount of publicity as the big funds, but it is in this segment of the market that the bulk of private equity transactions are completed. It is regarded by many participants as the most attractive part of the market to be in, a fact that is evidenced by the wide range of private equity funds describing themselves as "mid-market".

Finally, there are the early-stage investors who consider investing in start-ups or in the early years of a company's lifespan. These are the classic venture capitalists of yore. The reality is that this part of the market is very small relative to the mid-market and mega buyouts. Although there are many other sub-classifications, virtually all investors can be defined as mega, mid-market or early-stage.

ITS ECONOMIC IMPACT

Whichever class a private equity firm belongs to, evidence in the US and Europe suggests that the industry has played a key role in economic diversification, employment creation and value generation. One of the most comprehensive studies on this was completed by the British Venture Capital Association and IE Consulting, a specialist private equity research firm.[15]

It found that private equity-backed companies create jobs at a considerably faster rate than other private sector companies. Over the five years to 2003/4, the number of people employed in the UK by private equity-backed companies increased by an average of 20 per cent per annum, against a national private sector employment growth rate of 0.6 per cent. It is estimated that private equity-backed companies account for the employment of around 2.7 million people in the UK, equivalent to 18 per cent of UK private sector employment. It is also estimated that private equity-backed companies generated total sales of £187 billion and contributed around £23 billion in taxes.

15   *The Economic Impact of Private Equity in the UK (survey by British Venture Capital Association)*

It is these statistics that whet the appetites of political leaders in the Middle East. They would keenly welcome anything that generates a similar level of employment performance.

The performance of private equity-backed companies significantly strengthens the UK economy. Over the five years to 2003/4, private equity-backed companies' sales rose by an average of 23 per cent per annum, more than twice that achieved by FTSE 100 companies. Exports grew by 20 per cent per annum, compared with a national growth rate of just 3.3 per cent, and investment rose by five per cent per annum, compared with a national increase of 1.9 per cent.

PricewaterhouseCoopers and private equity firm 3i produce an annual report on private equity which has gained seminal status within the industry as a guide to its health and prosperity. The latest report, Global Private Equity 2004, tracks the state of the European market from complete 2003 figures. It makes illuminating reading for anyone seeking to gain an understanding of the industry's rising power.

During 2003, more than $115 billion of venture capital and private equity was invested, an increase of 33 per cent on the 2002 level and equal to 0.36 per cent of world gross domestic product. In 2003, private equity funds raised more than $82 billion, 12 per cent less than the $93 billion raised in 2002. The record year for fund-raising was 2000, when dotcom mania was at its height and global investors poured a staggering $160 billion into private equity funds. The slowdown in fund-raising since then should not be taken to mean that there is a lack of capital in the private equity market. According to the 3i/PwC report, the global overhang of funds raised over investments made between 1998 and 2003 stands at $211 billion. Of that total, $188 billion originated in North America and $39 billion in Europe.

Further evidence of the growth of the industry over the past quarter of a century can be gleaned by looking at the size of funds raised. In 1980, the world's largest fund, managed by Kohlberg Kravis Roberts out of New York, was just $135 million. Today, billion dollar funds are commonplace. Blackstone Group of the US is expected to close a $13 billion fund during 2006. The UK private equity industry raised £72 billion in 2004. If the industry continues on its present trajectory, by 2015 it may become a more important source of capital for companies than the London Stock Exchange.

THE EMERGING MARKETS PERSPECTIVE

Roger Leeds is a professor and director for International Business and Public Policy at Johns Hopkins University. He has a unique perspective that comes from being a former private equity investor who now dedicates his time to the study of it. This includes its role in emerging markets and he is chairman of the Emerging Markets Private Equity Association (EMPEA) which is rapidly becoming recognised as the global leader for information, data and applied research on private equity investing in emerging markets.

He says: "Private equity is already well established in the developed world. In the developing countries, private equity has a fundamentally important role to play in financing private sector growth and strengthening the local financial markets. Although the industry is in its infancy, it has begun to establish its credibility in emerging markets."

His point is well made. Investments in North America and Europe account for the great majority of private equity investments. Generally speaking the United States accounts for circa 50 per cent of all private equity activity. Much of the argument for the past two decades has focused on the returns available from backing private equity investors in those developed regions, but what about the next generation of deal opportunities further afield?

Historically, investors in Western-style private equity funds have been wary of backing even publicly listed companies in emerging markets – that is, if the laws were developed enough for foreigners to buy stocks in individual marketplaces. Political and economic risk dictates that investment in these areas is not for the fainthearted. It might be expected that investors would be even more wary therefore when dealing with illiquid holdings in private companies in emerging markets.

The question as to whether institutional investors – the pension funds and insurance companies that built private equity in the West – will do it in Asia, Africa and the Middle East as well is dependent on a number of uncertainties, such as the rule of law and corporate governance, relative to the developed markets.

Investors are already doing it in China and India where $15.4 billion of funds were raised in 2005 according to fresh research from **EMPEA**. Central, Eastern Europe and Russia accounted for a further $2.7 billion of funds raised in 2005 but the culture and mores of the Middle East make it a different environment in which to operate.

In fact the whole of Africa and the Middle East accounted for new funds valued at $962 million in 2005, an increase of 77 per cent on the year before. There are question marks over these numbers in the Middle East where industry practitioners and local research firms cite figures of around $2.5 billion as having been raised in 2005; irrespective of which figure is closest to the truth, the momentum is most definitely upwards.

Professor Leeds says: "My feeling today is that the private equity industry in the Middle East is developing in almost the opposite of other countries, both emerged and developing. Most private equity and venture capital start small. In this region, however, from the outset individual investments have been very large and practitioners are questioning whether there is too much capital given the capacity of deals."

EMPEA's strategy for the Middle East is to work with the leadership of the private equity industry to build a local organisation that will be closely aligned with **EMPEA** and serve as a model for effective collaboration between a global and a regional industry association. It would exist to deepen and broaden the market over a period of time. This would include liaising with governments, educating stakeholders about the role of private equity and generating data and research about the region.

For instance, EMPEA has begun to generate excellent research that has a real impact on the decision-making process. It has, at the time of going to press, released new research on what will influence limited partner investors to dedicate greater investment resource to emerging markets. It interviewed 76 respondents and asked, "How would these factors affect your interest in emerging markets private equity?"

	Significant increase	Moderate increase
• Greater reason for confidence in the accounting and corporate governance of emerging markets fund managers and portfolio companies	54%	38%
• Greater certainty that governments will implement sound economic policies	50%	45%
• Greater liquidity and a more reliable "IPO window" in local stock markets	38%	54%
• A significant improvement in returns over older vintage emerging markets funds	32%	57%
• Commitment by emerging markets fund managers to accepted reporting and valuation standards	34%	48%
• Greater investment by local institutions in emerging markets funds	9%	51%

These figures give a real mandate to today's general partners to prioritise the key elements of the process and do what is necessary to attract the next generation of investors. These numbers will be hugely influenced if leaders in the industry decide to enter the region.

Rumours abound that Blackstone and Carlyle, two of the greatest names in private equity today, are in deep discussions about launching funds for the Middle East. David Rubinstein, founder of Carlyle Group, recently joined the advisory board of the Emerging Markets Private Equity Association. Carlyle refused to be interviewed for this book. It was asked if speculation surrounding its plans to launch a private equity fund in the region was true and refused to be drawn on the subject. Our intelligence is that it will be launched in the final quarter of 2006 and first quarter of 2007. If true, they will compete for transactions with the likes of Abraaj Capital, the largest regional private equity firm in the Middle East, that some estimates suggest has built a 20% market share of private equity funds under management in the region allowing it to be the predominant local player.

What are the facts about emerging markets when it comes to private equity? There is no greater academic expert on the subject than Josh Lerner, the Jacob H. Schiff Professor of Investment Banking at Harvard Business School. He has written a plethora of books, articles and research papers on the subject of venture capital and private equity. His *Venture Capital and Private Equity: A Casebook* is seen by many as the seminal text on the subject.

In it there is a chapter on private equity in emerging markets which makes a number of fascinating points. Students of the subject should dedicate time to reading this worthy text, parts of which are accessible on the internet, but some of the key points he makes are:

There are four types of deals completed by private equity investors in developing markets. The first are privatisations. Many of these newly privatised enterprises are undercapitalized and desperately need to modernize. The simple distribution of shares to employees or others will not solve their need for financing. In many cases, the national capital markets are still not well developed, and access to international markets is limited to the largest firms. Consequently, governments and the private sector are turning to private equity to fill the investment gap.

A second market opportunity has been corporate restructurings. Globalisation has implied increased competition for many businesses in developing countries: lower trade barriers and new regulatory frameworks have forced companies to refocus their activities. Furthermore, the transfer of technologies and techniques from developed nations has provided new challenges, which existing management has often not been capable of meeting. Consequently, many private equity investments in developing nations have focused on either (i) purchasing and improving the operations of established firms or business units, or (ii) consolidating smaller businesses to achieve large, more cost-effective enterprises.

The final two categories of private equity investors are largely unique to the developing world. The first of these is investments in strategic alliances. In many cases, major corporations have made strategic investments (acquisitions, joint ventures, and alliances) in developing countries without a detailed knowledge of the business environment or their partners. To address these information gaps, corporations have increasingly welcomed private equity funds as third-party investors. The private equity investor is expected to provide much of the informed monitoring of the local partner that the corporation finds difficult to undertake.

A final class of investment has been infrastructure funds. Most infrastructure projects in the developed world have been financed through the issuance of bonds. In some developing nations, particularly in Asia, private equity funds have financed major projects, such as bridges, docks and highways.

Deal identification and due diligence. *In evaluating potential deals, however, private equity investors in developing nations emphasize two sets of risks often not encountered in developed nations. The first of these is country risk. A revolution, for instance, might lead to the nationalization of foreign investments.*

Deal structuring. *The choice of financing vehicle also differs between developed and developing markets. Investors in developed nations use a variety of instruments, including common and several classes of preferred stock, debt, and convertible preferred. These financial instruments allow the private equity investors to stage investments, allocate risk, control management, provide incentives to executives, and demarcate ownership. In many developing countries, private equity investors primarily use plain common stock. This reflects several factors. First, in several countries, especially in Asia, different classes of stock with different voting powers are not permitted. Thus, investors must seek other ways in which to control the firm. These are often of extreme importance, since most of the companies are family owned or controlled. Such control rights allow the venture capitalists to step in during such messy controversies such as a dispute between two sons as to who should succeed the father as president. While the structure of the investments may differ, shareholder agreements in developed and developing countries are likely to include the same control rights. These include affirmative covenants – such as the investors' right to access the firm's premises and records – as well as negative covenants that limit actions that the entrepreneur might take, such as the sale or purchase of significant assets of the firm. While the terms may be similar, their enforceability may vary. The enforceability of these shareholders' agreements depends strongly on the country or region of the investment.*

Pricing. *Significant differences also appear in the pricing of transactions in developed and developing nations. Venture capitalists' assessment of the value of a company in a developing nation is often problematic. Challenges abound at many levels. For instance, many developing countries lack timely and accurate macroeconomic and financial information. Sometimes macroeconomic variables published by central banks are manipulated by governments to portray a healthier economy. These uncertainties – combined with political and regulatory risk – may make it extremely difficult to draw up reasonably accurate projections. The uncertainty increases further since most private companies do not even have audited financial statements, especially family-run businesses. Furthermore, accounting principles and practices, although improving, are still very different from Western standards.*

FUTURE PERSPECTIVE FOR THE GLOBAL MARKET

The appendix at the end of the book provides a more detailed analysis of the key trends encompassing the global private equity industry – whereas the remainder of this book examines the key trends and issues facing private equity in the emerging markets of the Middle East.

The Western private equity industry today faces a range of challenges that it has not had to deal with before. Put simply, can it sustain its incredible returns during a period of increased competition and growing accountability – especially at a time when many leading funds are confronting internal succession issues and having to contend with the accompanying messy boardroom bust-ups that regularly pepper the financial pages coverage of the leading publicly listed companies?

It has become increasingly fashionable for industry commentators to suggest that there will be a small number of global leaders in the industry – firms such as Carlyle and Blackstone, which are fund-raising and investment machines – irrespective of the geography they elect to invest in. Others, meanwhile, will have to focus their expertise on specific industries or markets if they are to realise their potential.

Road-kill is already developing. Fortsmann Little, a famous name in the industry, has stated plans to close in 2006. A combination of misplaced investment decisions during the technology bubble and a failure to resolve its succession issues means this once great name is leaving the field. There are other hurdles too. These include an insatiable appetite from investors for improved returns at a time when competition for deal flow has never been higher, pushing up entry prices and thereby making it harder to generate exceptional returns. There is also a growing demand for improved accountability, particularly in the US, where there are calls for private equity firms to make public disclosures about the performance of their portfolio companies. Against this, industry practitioners argue that one of the reasons private equity is successful is that it is private. It is not subject to the short-term whims of quoted market fashion, so companies can adopt strategies designed to create value over the medium term.

Some say that private equity may, in time, become a victim of its own success. Techniques such as seeking to maximise cash flow, using debt astutely and paying managers with shares, which were novel when private equity firms first introduced them in the 1970s, have become standard business practice. The incentivisation techniques found in the private equity world are increasingly being seen in the quoted arena. As Henry Kravis said in a recent speech: "Everything we have accomplished in driving corporate excellence makes it harder for us to achieve the returns that our investors expect from us."

Success will be determined by whether private equity firms can genuinely improve the companies they buy and how easily they can dispose of their investments. Without an exit, there can be no profits. Two main exit routes – selling a firm to a big corporate buyer or floating it on a public stock market through an initial public offering of its shares – have recently been much harder to pursue than in the past. Popular alternatives, such as selling to another private equity firm, have attracted their fair share of controversy, with many observers questioning the sustainability of such approaches.

Much will depend on how investors respond to the new climate. Many have been disappointed by the average performance of the industry lately. However, as bonds and public equities continue to provide historically low yields, the high returns generated by the best private equity firms remain enticing. European institutional investors, which have traditionally invested only small amounts in private equity, are beginning to show more interest. If investors pump more capital into an industry that arguably already has too much of it, there is every chance of creating a private equity bubble.

Not only are good opportunities becoming harder to find, but as the industry matures other tricky issues emerge. Many of the leading private equity firms are still run by their founders, who are now getting to an age where they have to consider retirement. Some may linger too long. Even when they do leave, there is no guarantee that the next generation, clutching their MBAs, will inherit the deal-making magic of the founders.

It may be that private equity in the UK and the US has less to offer in the future than it has done in the past. This suggests that the real growth opportunities for the industry are more likely to be found in less developed markets, such as the Middle East.

In terms of key observations, the reality is that just as there is a twin-track economy in the region – the oil-rich Gulf able to expand more quickly than its neighbouring Levant – so, too, there are varying degrees of pace between the development of different private equity markets in the region.

Although it would be false to over-exaggerate the economic development of Saudi Arabia, Qatar, Egypt and the UAE, they are further down the journey – including in the evolution of private equity in their countries – than their neighbours. However the wider region is rapidly developing and a second edition of this text could well reference the evolution of funds in Turkey, Pakistan and Central Asia.

It is symptomatic of our times that enterprising investors are asking these questions at the very moment when returns in the developed markets of the United States and the UK are becoming so much harder to sustain.

Chapter 3

The quiet champions: the power of the regional trading families

RE-STRUCTURING TODAY: TRANSACTIONS TOMORROW?

"Please do not quote me. I want to help but you cannot mention my name or my company. We have a rule that says we must never give interviews."

So says a senior director within one of Saudi Arabia's many conglomerates. It employs in excess of 2,000 people, has operations across nine industries and is absolutely certain of one thing, it does not want to appear in the news or in the pages of a book that is examining the role of economics in the region.

This company is like so many other great trading families from within the region: instinctively conservative, utterly focused on nurturing a business for the long run rather than going after short term gains. The director says that times are demanding certain changes in attitude: "We have been going for hundreds of years in various guises. We are a trading group and, yes, we are considering all our options about what is the most appropriate structure for our future."

Investment bankers are never slow to bestow a code name for a transaction. Confidentiality requirements dictate that it makes sense, and so the industry is filled with "Project Falcon", "Project Nile", "Project Roadbridge" and "Project Blossom". These are not the code names for new stock market listings or for private company acquisitions. They are in fact the names that consultants and lawyers have given to the work they are doing on behalf of the family business owners.

For "project" read "restructuring".

Khaled Sheta is vice-chairman of the International Group of Companies in Egypt. It is a privately owned family business, albeit one which allows the occasional meeting with a financial journalist that has been operating for more than 30 years. It owns ten businesses across a range of industries.

Collectively the first nine generate aggregate sales of $300 million. The final business is a commodities unit that is involved in the trading of $700 million of assets per year. What is the topic discussed around the Sheta family dining table when talk turns to business?

He says: "Diversification is a strategy that has historically made sense. If you are in ten industries you are able to iron out the different developments ongoing in each industry and so maximise your opportunities. But now we find ourselves operating in a global market and having to compete against specialised players."

Globalisation has resulted in many changes, whether one is operating in the United States, United Kingdom or United Arab Emirates, but one that has gone largely unreported to date is the impact on family businesses in the Arab world.

There is no research on the true size and value of companies owned by this group, but it is known to run into the hundreds of billions of dollars. They are collectively some of the most financially powerful people in the world. However, these businesses have been nurtured over centuries in some cases and decades in others and consequently operate to a different rhythm.

Khalid Abunayyan of the eponymous water and energy group in Saudi Arabia says: "We are not interested in the short-term gains of the stock market. Everything that we do is built upon the premise of going after sustainable long-term growth."

These trading families have built their position by blending commercial nous with an ability to generate opportunities from their relationships with the ruling families. Consequently they have built significant businesses, which are now confronted by major questions that will impact on their future long-term well-being.

When HH Prince Fahad Bin Abdullah talks about government's need to examine its assets and then go through a three-pronged process of corporatise, commercialise and privatise, he is directing his message as much to members of his family business as to the government. This quest to blend tradition with modernity, one of the chief challenges facing the region, is what is driving the restructuring debates.

SUCCESSION MANAGEMENT: THE BURNING ISSUE INSIDE THE FAMILIES

Getting it wrong will have terrible consequences for some of the region's great businesses. Businesses that have been built over generations develop an immune system against anything that might harm them. But issues surrounding succession do have the potential to attack the body politic of a family and destroy value in the business. Just listen to the region-wide sigh of relief that greeted the resolution of issues surrounding the future of Kuwait in February 2006 as further evidence of how fragile some of these families can be and how all attention is focused on the next round of succession.

Large-scale family enterprises are hardly a Gulf-specific phenomenon. It is estimated that family owned enterprises account for over two-thirds of business enterprises worldwide and around one-third of Fortune 500 companies.

Given their predominance in the Gulf region, the critical issues facing these entities are adequate planning for succession management, clear rules for corporate governance and clear vision on governance issues related to distinguishing between ownership and management.

Abdullah Mouallimi spent two decades working within the Olayan Group, the leading Saudi Arabian trading family, before leaving to set up his own business in 1997. Olayan is seen by many as one of the finest examples of a trading family business. His entrepreneurial career was broken by a four-year period as mayor of Jeddah and he remains chairman of the Jeddah Chamber of Commerce.

He says: "Restructuring is itself a code word for the chief issue facing the families. This is succession planning." Currently he provides consulting to a number of the leading families throughout the region, albeit refusing to divulge their names. "What do they want to talk about? Organisational structures, joint venture agreements and how to develop in the domestic and international business community."

John Davis, author of *Challenges Facing Family Companies in the Gulf Region*, says, "What are the common issues? Succession, sibling issues, branch rivalries. You find perennial issues such as, 'How do we deal with the family relying too much financially on the business, because family dependence can drain the very life out of the business', and 'How do we develop the next generation successfully? Those are universal concerns."

He continues that the fast-changing role of the state in Gulf economies suggests "family companies in the Gulf region have to become much more performance-driven if they are going to survive long-term. What you hope for is that there's a good partnership between the family and non-family managers so that they can be of like mind in the management of the company".

Open a copy of a Western newspaper, and every day there will be business stories about tensions in the boardroom at leading companies. Family businesses in the Middle East are better at keeping their affairs private, but every so often splits happen that can have significant impact.

In the small Sultanate of Oman is a very large company, the Bahwan Group. It was originally set up by Suhail and Saud Bahwan in 1965 with a single shop selling fishing nets, watches and building materials in the Muttrah Souk. A successful attempt to win the licence for Toshiba and Seiko in 1968 and 1969 transformed the business and enabled them to create the process whereby many further licences were subsequently obtained including Toyota. By 2001 the group had grown into one of Oman's largest businesses, with diversified interests across a range of sectors.

For reasons that are difficult to unearth, although believed to be driven by differences in opinion about the future strategy of the group, the brothers decided to split the business in 2001 and each set forth on individual strategies. Saud Bahwan took control of its automotive interests including the franchise for Toyota in Oman and Suhail took charge of its other interests. Suhail Bahwan's business interests have a collective turnover of in excess of $1 billion and include stakes in the National Bank of Oman and a number of other privatisation projects.

Despite the fact that Suhail's four children all work inside the business, the nature of the 2001 split has raised the spectre of what can potentially go wrong if succession is not managed effectively. Consequently the business is believed to be considering its options in relation to a public listing over the next few years for one or more of its portfolio companies.

The Bahwan Group is not the only one to have split in recent years. Majid and Abdullah Al Futtaim who together built the most successful commercial enterprise in the Emirates had a very public splitting of the portfolio a few years ago and it is reported that the Galadari group is undergoing similar stresses at present following the death of Abdullatif Galadari, the last of four brothers who built a once mighty business in the same country. The Mannai Group in Qatar, the second generation Juffali brothers in Saudi Arabia and the Moayyed family in Bahrain have all experienced degrees of separation over the last few years.

WHAT DOES RESTRUCTURING ACTUALLY MEAN IN PRACTICE?

For Arab business families, what does a decision to restructure actually mean?

Sheta says: "We have just begun the process of internally restructuring and have in-house advisers. So we are talking about devising appropriate legal structures, making our businesses a little more independent and creating an over-arching holding company with appropriate management inside it. Then there is the financial restructuring to think about. This may involve reconfiguring the debt requirements of a business, using equity, thinking about private equity and listing shares."

It is no wonder the advisory community is so busy.

Businesses that are built on a philosophy of nurturing subsidiaries are having to retain that philosophy but leap-frog a series of transitions to make the businesses competitive for a global environment. The spirit of the family may still be most relaxed in the desert at weekends, but it needs to move its structure closer to a New York listed entity if it is to compete on the increasingly global stage of business.

Sheikh Abdulrahman Ali Al Turki is chairman of Al Turki Trading Corporation and one of the most respected business leaders in Saudi Arabia. He is viewed as a classic example of a shrewd individual who slowly built a diversified business over many decades. The oil services business has been good to him and his family and enabled him to diversify into a range of sectors. The jovial pragmatist is unlikely to be hurried by anybody, but speaking from his central London office, he recognises the need to respond to the times.

He says: "ATCO may consider a flotation on the stock market in a few years. Why? For continuity of the business. We are not talking to any banks to help us. We depend on ourselves. Maybe in the future. If we were to list, we would have to develop those relationships, but not yet."

That was all he was willing to say on the subject. But the words "continuity of the business" are the fundamental reason for driving change amongst the families. A blend of personal reputation, family honour and straightforward financial requirements dictates that these businesses take their feet out of the mid-20th century and long-jump into the 21st. This is likely to generate huge amounts of activity and have a domino effect throughout the region.

WHO THEY ARE AND WHERE THEY CAME FROM

The following is a list of just some of the families in the region who are likely to be in the process of constantly reviewing and considering the most effective and efficient structures by which they should operate. Our chapter feature at the end of this section provides a more detailed overview of these families.

Country	Family
Oman	Bahwan
Saudi Eastern Province	Al Turki
Saudi Riyadh	Olayan
Saudi Jeddah	Al Juffali
Qatar	Al Fardan
UAE Abu Dhabi	Al Fahim
UAE Dubai	Al Futtaim
Egypt	Sawaris
Kuwait	Al Kharafi
Bahrain	Kanoo
Jordan	Masri
Lebanon	Hariri

There is a separate book to be written on the history of each of these families. In their own way they are local – albeit smaller – versions of the European Rothschilds or American Carnegies. Most can trace their trading origins to the 19th century, some earlier, when the sea trade with India and East Africa provided opportunities for an enterprising group of early stage entrepreneurs. Some began importing, others facilitated, but each instigated the beginnings of large dynasties.

Most families truly began to make their mark post-World War II with the emergence of the vast oil reserves. Many of today's leaders owe their success to providing energy services at a domestic or international level and seeing their fortunes rise and fall with the value of an oil barrel.

As trade and the requirement to service growing populations grew, and as consumer markets began to ramp up, the region saw the emergence of another layer of family enterprise whose core equities lie in their acquisition of vast distribution, representation, franchise and licensing rights.

Families such as Al-Juffali in Saudi Arabia began to represent over 60 major Western brand owners, like Michelin, Siemens and even the mighty IBM. They also became enormous Daimler Benz agents (at one stage, importing more Daimler Benz trucks than any other market in the world). The Alghanims in neighbouring Kuwait became the biggest overseas distributors of General Motors cars and trucks over that period.

In the Gulf, families like Al Futtaim, Al Naboodah, Al Ghurair, Al-Habtoor, Galadari and Al-Tayer emerged in the 1960s and later, to acquire the bulk of the UAE's vast automotive, construction, consumer goods, media representation and luxury retail distribution rights and to make vast fortunes in the process.

Often these lucrative concessions came at the behest of ruling families, who themselves now recognised the enormous wealth in their own hands, through their vast real estate and other asset holdings. They in turn began – principally in the 1990s – to recognise the opportunity to step into the private arena themselves and to unlock value by partnering with the private sector to carve up and exploit their own holdings.

So whilst key assets remained in the hands of the state and the public sector, the emergence of groups like Dubai Land, Dubai Investment Company and Emaar Properties saw the evolution of head of state or crown prince as effective CEO, or at least the principal source of power behind a tier of pioneering and entrepreneurial (local) executive managers.

There is a sliver of irony every time aides to President Bush portray him as America's chief executive officer. The Texan oil man likes nothing more than to portray himself as leader of the world's number one company. Cynics use the moniker to mock. But the reality is that, although it is never stated, the rulers in the Middle East are very much the chief executive officers of companies that do control incredible assets and material wealth.

The biggest corollary of this process of growth has been the internal tensions within family groups to modernise and recognise their true value and potential at the expense of family members whose main source of income has – in some cases – come with relatively little effort attached.

"Family and succession management" is a recurring theme in the region, as corporatised players in the financial services and investment banking sectors have sought to tap into what is clearly a major source of liquidity and assets, from an often under-exploited and under-leveraged source.

The private nature of the families means that there is very limited financial information available to rank their performance. Because their assets are spread among so many different markets, it is further complicated.

Attempts have been made in the past to assess their input to regional society. In 1985, more than 20 years ago, Michael Field, a leading journalist who has covered the region, wrote a book called *The Merchants: The Big Business Families of Saudi Arabia and the Gulf States*. He followed this up a decade later with a seminal work, *Inside the Arab World*.

Focusing on one family in particular gives a deeper opportunity to examine the pioneering spirit which resonates throughout the region. The Olayan family of Saudi Arabia engender respect and a loyal following from all those who have had active dealings with them and are living proof of a long established way of doing business the right way. They are managing to cross the bridge from the past to the future, with Lubna Olayan sitting as a non-executive director of WPP, the global marketing communications company.

By understanding the history of this company it is possible to get a sense of why the trading families represent the bridge between the Arab philosophy towards business in the 20th century and the rapidly evolving outlook in this one.

Today's Olayan Financing Company of Saudi Arabia is a holding and management arm for more than 70 separate business units. Visitors to its website are confronted by a daunting anthem to introduce the company's global operations. These are split in three. Saudi operations are an umbrella term for 11 business units focused on delivering products and services to Saudi Arabia. These cover commercial, industrial, real estate development, hotels and tourism, transportation and freight, consumer goods and the IT sector. In real terms it has the Saudi rights to Coca-Cola, Burger King, Colgate toothpaste and Nestlé chocolates.

The global investing arm will take stakes in public and private equity funds plus fixed income bonds. It seeks to invest in companies with high-quality assets, secure cash flow, conservative leverage, high liquidity, well-structured borrowing, a transparent culture and effective fiscal controls. Located in Athens, the business manages the overall exposure of the group to investment opportunities.

Strategic Alliances is the third leg of the business and is focused on striking agreements with world-leading companies to offer their products and services in Saudi Arabia. It is not known how many billions of dollars the combined entity is currently worth, but its significance prompted *Arabian Business* magazine to place Lubna Olayan, the daughter of its founder, Suliman Saleh Olayan, who today oversees much of it on a day-to-day basis, as the fourth most powerful person in the Arab world.

The story of how this business was built from a single unit – General Contracting Company – in 1947 to its magnificence today is an astonishing tale of entrepreneurship, shrewd judgement and an insatiable appetite for work.

Suliman Olayan has been described by many as the Warren Buffett of the Middle East. It is not sycophantic to say he was even better as he was an operator first and investor second.

His entrepreneurial career began in 1947 when he obtained a small contract from Bechtel to supply transportation services on the Trans-Arabian pipeline between Saudi Arabia and Lebanon. He delivered a good job that was on time and on budget in a professional fashion. As with all entrepreneurs, who only need their single break to instigate the momentum that allows them to get going, he leveraged this single contract and the work that was completed. Marketing to many firms in the region as a consequence of the construction boom of the late 1940s and early 1950s, he was able to develop rapidly from having a small team of contractors into growing a genuine business.

He remained resolutely focused on his construction business but was shrewd enough to see how the country was developing. The infrastructure requirements were huge and so he tentatively decided to diversify during the 1950s by developing Saudi Arabia's earliest electrical power companies. He founded the country's first public utility, the National Gas Company, a distributor of propane gas.

In 1954, he launched General Trading Company (GTC), the Group's food and consumer products distribution business. During the early 1950s he began to realise the need to put some downside protection on his assets in the event of something going wrong. The process of sourcing insurance was not as simple as he felt it should be. So in classic entrepreneurial terms, he set up his own version of an insurance company that delivered in the image he felt it should. Arab Commercial Enterprises (ACE) was set up in 1954 which went on to become the largest insurance and reinsurance broker in the Middle East. In the 1960s, Suliman turned to international equity investing, an activity which would eventually establish the Group as an influential participant in global capital markets.

At all times he and his colleagues were nurturing their existing businesses whilst developing future revenue streams. Meantime, Suliman was also developing business alliances, pioneering in Saudi Arabia the concept of "strategic partnerships" long before this term became commonplace.

He kept up his relationship to Bechtel. Moreover, through GTC and GCC he acquired exclusive distributorships from Kimberly-Clark, General Foods, Pillsbury, Hunt Wesson, Cummins Engine, Kenworth and Atlas Copco. In 1969, the Group obtained a licence from Kimberly-Clark to construct the first paper tissue converting plant in Saudi Arabia. Also that year, GTC established one of the first cold storage and meat processing plants in the Kingdom and the Group played a leading role with other Saudi and foreign investors to establish a large factory for manufacturing plastic pipes and fittings. Other joint manufacturing ventures with major multinationals followed.

In the late 1980s, the Group began to undertake a series of new activities in Saudi Arabia, particularly in light of manufacturing and franchising, reaching beyond the Kingdom to other Gulf countries and the greater Middle East. At the same time, it consolidated and strengthened existing operations, a process that continues.

Internationally, the Group has built upon Suliman's reputation as an astute and prudent investor. Today the Group's substantial international holdings include fixed income securities, public equities, private equities and real estate. These investments are concentrated in but not limited to the US and Europe. In addition, the Group has substantial real estate holdings in America and Britain.

There is something very special about the long-term perspective that the trading families bring to bear on the businesses they own and run. Suliman belonged to the first generation, but how has the challenge been taken up by other families that have already successfully transitioned into the second generation?

"Get in the cab and tell it to go towards the Holiday Inn on the Old Airport Road. Opposite the Holiday Inn is the Islamic Affairs building. There is a building next to it, under the Gulf Bridge. That is where we are but here is my mobile if you get lost," says Khalid Abunayyan. How many board directors of businesses with annualised sales of more than $500 million do you know who would take the time to give that much context to a meeting?

Khalid, general manager of the company launched by his father 55 years ago, is eager to give the perspective on what is really happening inside the trading families. It becomes one of the most fascinating interviews of all those undertaken during the research. The boardroom of the Abunayyan empire, in their Riyadh headquarters, is filled with certificates, awards and trophies, many related to the sporting endeavours of the group's various teams.

The business was started by his father, Abdullah Abunayyan, who had no formal education but was exceptionally shrewd when it came to the building of a business. Abdullah Abunayyan was working for his father, a merchant, who brought foodstuffs from India and the Gulf, but wanted to do something on his own.

His initial venture was the introduction of the agricultural pump to the country. Previously, farmers had relied on animals to pump water and he saw the use of technology to improve upon it. He struggled to begin with, persuading farmers to swap their old ways for the new, but he overcame their issues and successfully sold it. Over many years, he slowly began a process of diversifying into other areas such as desalination, power plants and waste and water. And so 55 years later the main focus is on water and power.

Fast forward to today and the business is a medium-sized company. It employs 1,500 people and has got to this point through a philosophy of focusing on long term sustainable growth. Whereas many in the region are keener to play the markets for short-term gains, this is a business that is built on strong long-term future prospects.

Khalid Abunayyan highlights a number of factors behind the developing success of Saudi Arabia: "There are geopolitical reasons. The Saudi government has dealt with internal security threats. They have done this very well and our intelligence has improved a lot. Secondly, political reforms are growing. The press will today discuss hot issues that it would not face a few years ago. I am encouraged by economic reforms as well. There have been a number of privatisations, such as Saudi Telecom, and lots of opportunities in water and power projects as well."

These reforms are having a direct impact on the ground. He highlighted the ACWA Power Developments business as an example of what can happen in the modern Saudi Arabia. This business has now begun two multi-billion dollar projects that are examples of what can happen when public and private sectors come together.

The first is an integrated water and power project 80 kilometres south of Jeddah. The consortia will build, own and operate the site and the total investment will be $2.5 billion.

This project will be 32 per cent owned by the Saudi Public Investment Fund, eight per cent owned by the Water & Electricity Company and 60 per cent owned by a consortium that includes Abunayyan Group, two Malaysian investors and some private backers.

A second project costing $1.5 billion is the Saudi Aramco Sumitomo Petrochemical complex currently being built. ACWA will be supplying this complex with water, power and steam. These are huge projects that would not have been structured as they have just a few years ago. The government is using experts and ensuring that projects that will have sustainable benefits are being built.

Khalid Abunayyan says the plan is to float ACWA Power on the Saudi stock market in three years. He says: "Our focus must be Saudi first as our prime responsibility is to share the wealth with the general Saudi public. It [the plan is to float ACWA Power on the Saudi stock market in three years] will be a multi-billion issue and we will work with local, national and international firms."

Many advisers will view this as a key test case of whether the family wants to adopt the mores of the 21st century and consider a listing. Abunayyan says: "Part of the government's changes has been to put systems in place to liberate regulations, putting the Capital Markets Authority in place, which has opened up a whole new opportunity for businesses such as ours. We can now tap into the capital markets as a source of funding."

Other reforms that he recommends the government considers launching relate to the entry and exit of foreign nationals for work purposes "The first prime requirement is to make it easy for people to come in and enter the country. Our visa system is very difficult and it is not working. We need to be more inviting. The first time anybody makes a judgment on Saudi Arabia is when they visit our embassies overseas and I do not think the experience is good enough. We can sometimes be a little too conservative and concerned about other issues that may not actually be there."

He also highlights the importance of women in the workplace. "They [women in the work-place] are a productive part of our system. The labour laws have been written to protect the rights of male and female workers. We employ one woman out of 1,500 and we are seriously considering changes in our finance, administration and marketing departments to generate more employment for women. It must make pure economic sense but women will be a big boost to the economy. There are some jobs that will not be occupied by men. Women in some areas are better than men. They are more disciplined, productive and will add value.

There are a lot of women who are widows, divorcees, living on welfare, taking care of their parents and I honestly think that we should create economic opportunities for them. There is Al Nahdha Charity Organization which provides employment placement services to women. They do it for charity reasons. It is female only workers. There are more and more duplication of this experience. I will give you another good example. All sales people in female retail stores must become women over the next 18 months. Those jobs used to be occupied by non Saudi men and within 18 months, it will be Saudi women. This is Saudisation at work for the best."

Whether Saudi Arabia, rather than Dubai, will be the long-term economic hub for the region remains to be seen. It is a question that all Saudis have a perspective on. "They have approached it in a different way and are doing well. A lot of foreign companies have capitalised on the openness of Dubai, but they are there as a base to do business in Saudi Arabia. I see no reason why Saudi Arabia will not become an economic hub for the region."

But are international businesses not scared off by Saudi Arabia's reputation?

"We have gone through a very difficult phase following September 11th. I praise our government for taking a number of very wise steps and have put our issues out on the table. But the West must understand that terrorism is an international problem. There is a major responsibility to examine the sources of extremism. Many in the Middle East are impoverished, uneducated and have nothing to look forward to. Just look at some of the Palestinians. What future do they have? Once that is dealt with, there will be great stability in the region. We all have a social, economic and political responsibility to make it work."

The changes that are being completed inside the families are shifting the nature of their relationships with private equity operators. Historically it was a simple relationship. These families would invest in American and European funds as part of a sensible diversification strategy.

One founder of a $1bn US buyout fund says: "The reality is that the region represents a fraction of our fundraising needs. The lion's share comes from US and European institutions, but I do like dealing with the region. The people at the highest levels are very smart and know what they are doing. They are good investors to have."

Time is never wasted when it is spent with the business elite of the region, for it provides a fascinating window on the key trends that are enveloping the market place. Abdulmohsen Al-Touq, of the eponymous trading company, oversees a business that incorporates 15 subsidiaries across a range of assets. Each company is independent and tries to recruit the best of breed managers to run its component parts, operating to the highest levels of corporate governance.

So what are the chief challenges facing the families in the region? "The need to institutionalise our operations," he says. "When a family with assets of $30m sees the assets grow as a consequence of increased price of oil to $500m there is a totally different business to be run and that means having the infrastructure to do it."

This has raised a number of issues related to the rise of the capital markets. "People drool over the returns from the stock market," he says. "They are depending on it. They are neglecting their own business to focus on the market. That is becoming scary. Markets are clearly inflated and these people will get hurt. But there is a flip side. The growth in the capital markets is encouraging entrepreneurship. People are starting restaurants, shops and getting excited by the potential to grow."

The natural inclination of families to diversify means they continue to be key investors in a range of private equity funds. Al-Touq believes this will continue over the coming years. "We are active investors in it. It provides smart diversification for us. We invest in local and regional operators as well as in the big international funds."

It is this exposure to private equity investing that has led to changes in how Al-Touq and a number of other family members review their holdings. He says: "We have one company which must remain nameless. We have spent much of the past year in talks with other groups, that own similar or complimentary businesses. We think there are many synergies and value add by merging our various interests together to create a larger, diversified and more cost effective business. This is using a mixture of mergers to build a larger platform. Private equity firms would describe this as a 'club deal' or a 'buy and build', but whatever it is called, it seems to make sense to us. At the end of the day the market is full of opportunities. Some of them are more complexed and would require a lot of work, but if done right, the rewards are very promising."

This is further evidence of the growing trend to distinguish and separate ownership and the founders from management. He says: "It has always been a philosophy that the managers must have alignment with the owners. The management do have options and are given a career path to allow them to participate in the success of the company. To attract the right people, you have to give them a share of the pie."

Abdulmohsen Al-Touq is just another example of how traditional trading families are morphing into new structures – they are witnessing the catapulting rise of local equity markets and the rise of private equity and reacting accordingly. Attitudes are changing. The restructuring of family offices is a natural prequel to discussions about deals.

To private equity investors such as Yasser El Mallawany, chairman and chief executive of Egypt's EFG Hermes, they represent a definite source of finance for their funds and a possible source of deals. "The abundance of capital in the region means that we do not have to go elsewhere," he says.

There is nothing new about private equity investors both from within and outside the region coming to it for capital. As Khalid Abunayyan says: "Private equity investors provide diversification. It is common sense to use them. Frankly the Dubai and Saudi stock markets are over-valued and it is about making investments within the context of your attitudes to risk and return." But could the trading families actually become sources of deal flow as well as capital?

As more and more funds are launched, this is likely – or so the logic goes – to make the sourcing of opportunities ever harder. The list of potential sources of deal flow has changed little over the years. It includes the purchase of stakes in privatisations, the acquisition of businesses from expatriate business owners and also the purchase of assets currently owned by traditional trading families.

Frederic Sicre, an executive director of Abraaj Capital, says: "Obviously we all have our own networks in the region and beyond. But ultimately the deals come from government, local trading families or expatriate business owners."

The irony is not lost on anyone with a historical interest in the region. The very people – the Arab trading families – who are now seen as a potential source of deal flow to fuel the future development of private equity in the region can actually be viewed in certain terms as its pioneers.

It does not take much research into the psyche of the traditional trading family to realise that they do not like selling and prefer building. They nurture businesses rather than manage for the short term; however, they have built up cross-market and cross-sector portfolios of assets which are certainly equivalent to Western-style conglomerates and are viewed by many as quasi-private equity portfolios.

To sell, or to be seen to sell, is not really an option. Creative structures that allow them to build their businesses are much more palatable. However, it is worth contrasting the Middle East with Western Europe. According to a recent research study, family enterprises accounted for 37 per cent, 31 per cent and 29 per cent of the volume of 2002 buyouts in France, Germany and Switzerland respectively, with deals including the acquisition of the German Auto-Teile-Unger by Doughty and Vendome Group in France by 3i being notable examples of the phenomenon.

The same issues and neurosis that influence the thinking of family businesses across the globe are as applicable in Kuwait and Bahrain as they are in France and Germany. But just as those Western Europeans have revised and updated their thinking, so too will those in the Middle East.

This book believes that the great Arab trading families have played a fundamental role in the development of the Middle East in general and the Gulf in particular. They have provided a stable environment to nurture generations of managers and employees, instituted a culture that invests in businesses to allow them to fulfil their potential and encouraged innovation in their domestic and regional markets.

Longevity of itself is not a defining characteristic for the world's greatest businesses. However the world's leading companies are able to manage simultaneously for the long- and short-term. Consequently they build sustainable businesses which can outlive the personality of their founder. This ability to manage for the short and long term underpins the personality of the businesses developed by the regional trading families.

Names such as Olayan and Al Zamil in Saudi Arabia, Kanoo in Bahrain and Al Futtaim in the UAE engender huge respect for the manner in which they have built, extended and developed their businesses over the past decades. Each has a sprawling set of interests, across a range of sectors and regions.

Go to the websites of some of these great trading families today and it is as if you are examining a portfolio of private equity holdings. Because these families are the pioneers of multiple company ownership in the Middle East, they are the pioneers of private equity.

Sheikh Sultan Bin Saqr Al Qassimi, founder of GIBCA, a leading UAE construction business that represents an example of a great local trading family's business success, says: "Trading families do discuss what is happening in private equity. They recognise they have portfolios of assets and are thinking about how best to maximise their value. But they do not like to sell, certainly not to other families or private purchasers. The stock market is a more attractive option."

However, there are some tentative signs that this attitude is changing: Sheikh Khaled Al Nahyan is the founder of the Bin Zayed Group of companies that he launched in 1988 after completing his business studies in America. Today the business encompasses a range of diversified interests, employs 2,000 people, and continues to grow apace.

"I have done two things that marks me out from what others say in the region," he says. "I have failed and I am willing to sell."

Failure refers to an investment in FastTV, a US online video company that burned through $10 million of investment before the life-support machine was turned off. "We were too early for the business. We tried to do video on the net and it didn't work at that time due to bandwidth issues." Meanwhile, he also says: "I will sell any business that I can get the right price for. Business is fun. It is about having an idea, creating the business and moving on."

This attitude, though refreshing, is unusual, says Makram Kubeisy, managing director of the investment banking advisory business at Shuaa Capital: "Culturally, people do not want to sell the family jewels. Especially the older generation. An outright sell is not sexy. But the second point is: 'What would they do with the cash?'"

Actually, so the argument goes, you create a further headache for them if they sell. As things currently stand, these families have a deep understanding of their businesses, the risks involved and the return they get. Even if it makes intellectual sense to sell, that process becomes a catalyst for reinvestment headaches as they would have to determine what to do with a large cheque.

Visitors to economics conferences can see that the people who are speaking are getting ever younger and more attuned to this approach. It might just be true that family businesses are undertaking restructuring today that will lead to transactions tomorrow.

THE NEW ERA

The family is the key to business life in the Gulf region. More than 95 per cent of all businesses are family owned and most economic activity in the private sector is dominated by a handful of large, family-run conglomerates.

Their rise to prominence over the past 50 years is intrinsically linked, in almost every case, to the discovery and exploitation of oil reserves or to long-standing relationships with the ruling families of the region.

But external pressures and the need to become more competitive on the international stage are driving change within these groups. And there is a growing belief among academics, management consultants and other external experts that the way in which a few key families have dominated commercial life in the Gulf and the Levant will, inevitably, change, as the founders and first-generation descendants of the great business enterprises, retire and pass power to their sons.

Recently published research by Wharton Professor Raphael Amit and Harvard Business School Professor Belen Villalonga suggests that while family run businesses may be the best bet for stakeholders as long as the founder remains involved as chief executive officer or chairman, value is invariably lost if a descendant runs the company.

History proves too that descendants may not be the best people to run their fathers' and grandfathers' businesses. Amin Nasser, a partner at PricewaterhouseCoopers, says: "Only six per cent [of family businesses] survive to the third generation, and fewer than two per cent survive to the fourth. Bringing in outside talent will be required to maintain the survival of long-established businesses."

Furthermore, many family-run businesses may need to raise external capital in order to survive in the modern world. To do so, they can list on the public markets, divest non-core operations or break themselves up completely and float or sell off different divisions. Several major companies, such as Dubai's Emirates airline, which is owned by the ruling al-Maktoum family, and Qatar's Al-Jazeera satellite news channel, owned by the ruling al-Thani family, have said they are considering initial public offerings.

Emirates requires funds to finance its rapid expansion, with the arrival of one new aircraft every month for the next five to six years. Sheikh Ahmed Saeed al-Maktoum, chairman of Emirates, said that the owners of the airline were "always talking about an initial public offering". A spokesman for Al-Jazeera said the idea of privatising the news channel had been raised by the Emir of Qatar. Currently its budget is covered by the Qatari authorities and advertising revenues. The station's board has now been tasked with drawing up a report within the next year on the best method of transforming the station into a company with private participation.

But there is a big difference between the privatisations of the ruling families and the development of the trading families.

Salman Deghaithar, a senior executive at Gulf International Bank, says family-run businesses should consider selling shares to investors sooner rather than later. "If they wait for problems to happen and make the transition under pressure, they will lose the confidence of banks and financial markets," he said. "Family businesses will grow and be able to obtain bank loans to finance their expansion" if they turn into publicly traded companies, he added.

Mr Deghaithar said that this option is increasingly popular among younger generations, which are keen to crystallise their wealth and pursue other interests. There are more than 1,200 living descendants of Al Sabah in Kuwait, for example, while the Galadari Group is run by four brothers, none of whom is powerful enough to buy out his siblings.

David Jackson, executive vice-president at the Dubai-based investment holding company Istithmar, believes that families "have to do a lot of soul-searching." He suggests that they should think about commissioning reports from management consultants who can help them work out where their core interests lie. Consultants and international investment banks can also help businesses to evaluate their true worth.

As these groups stand on the cusp of a new era, the private equity industry should be ideally placed to assist them. Private equity firms can provide viable exits with minimum risk to reputation. Because the money and management expertise comes through a third-party financial institution rather than a rival corporation, emotive issues of family pride and rivalry become far less important.

"We are faceless," says Abraaj chief executive Arif Naqvi, who is almost always credited with having pioneered professional private equity investing in the region. "The people we approach do not feel threatened. Private equity is a solution for the expatriate owner, for family succession, and for the company looking to move to the next level."

In addition, private equity groups can act for family businesses by identifying acquisition targets or international partners for their core businesses or service areas. They can then work with the family enterprises to make such acquisitions. In particular, they might be able to act as a catalyst where regional businesses have set up partnerships with multinational corporations and are now seeking to generate transactions on a local basis. This process can be helped in particular by family groups who are awash with ready liquidity and interested in deal-making but do not have the requisite level of skill at financing, structuring and exiting transactions.

At present, there remain a number of cultural obstacles preventing private equity firms from playing a larger role in the evolution of family businesses. In particular, the sale of an unprofitable enterprise to a rival group is still widely viewed as a sign of failure and not an ideal option.

Understandably, family groups often want to keep problems to themselves. As David Knights, private equity director at HSBC says: "A question I used to hear a lot, and still do occasionally, which summed up the problem was: 'If the business is any good, why are you selling it?'"

Nonetheless, there is a view that some family groups appear to be coming closer and closer to taking the plunge. There is evidence of a generational change in the management of family businesses that has thrown up young, dynamic entrepreneurs educated in Western business schools. The process of change is slow, but it is happening.

How the families bring their business structures into the 21st century will be one of the chief stories of the financial landscape over the next decade. The Middle East is culturally distinctive, so it will evolve at its own pace. But market economics knows no boundaries and the region is not insulated from the key trends that impact on conglomerates around the world.

The need to focus so as to maximise the effectiveness of a business has become an underlying tenet of company valuation in the West. As the regional stock markets continue to develop, there is likely to be an ever-growing appetite from the trading families to consider listing their assets – or partial stakes – so as to receive a liquid valuation and acquisition currency. The landscape is changing. So, too, will the trading families.

CHAPTER FEATURETTE
– The trading families: mini profiles

Saudi Eastern Province

Al Turki Group (ATCO)

Abdulrahman Ali Al Turki launched his independent business career in 1976. Thirty years later he is listed in *Arabian Business* magazine as one of the 50 most powerful Arabs in the world. He sits atop, as the 100 per cent equity owner, a conglomerate that is composed of 23 different subsidiaries. It is structured into four core subsidiaries.

AA Turki Corporation for Trading and Contracting owns assets in a range of infrastructure and oil services businesses. It has a second arm – structured as a series of limited liability companies – in which Sheikh Abdulrahman owns a majority or material amount of the equity, such as its holding in the Saudi Danish Construction Corporation. The third leg to this Saudi conglomerate is its joint ventures. These include a deal with Honeywell. Finally there are a series of wholly owned offshore business units in the United States and United Kingdom.

Al Zamil

More than 8,000 people are employed by this Saudi conglomerate, whose mantra is "strength through diversity." It is composed of more than 45 companies across the world. The business began in the 1930s when the late Sheikh Abdullah Al-Hamad Al Zamil established a modest trading entity selling food items and textiles in the Kingdom of Bahrain. This evolved quite quickly into real estate in Saudi Arabia.

Unusually for a conglomerate in the Middle East, it is willing to disclose a limited amount of financial information. Its website outlines some very basic figures for 2000, 2001 and 2002, which indicates how often it updates its brochure to the world.

Its core business lines are in petrochemicals, industrial and consumer products and it has a range of other assets. These include financial investments in a range of regional and international assets.

Saudi Riyadh

The Olayan Group

The Olayan family remains one of the most influential in the region and internationally. A dynasty – one that is seen by many as having the best management techniques of all the regional conglomerates – it is able to produce a stream of brilliant executives, who go on to great things both within and outside the organisation.

Today, Olayan Investment Company Establishment, the parent company, is headed by Lubna Olayan, the daughter of the late Suliman Olayan, who is seen by many as the most influential female in the Arab world. She oversees a conglomerate that has interests in more than 40 companies generating sales that run into the billions of dollars.

Away from business she is an active member of the World Economic Forum, where she is a member of the Arab Business Council Executive Committee. She is also a member of the Board of Trustees of the Arab Thought Foundation, a think-tank based in Beirut.

Saudi Jeddah

Al Juffali Group

Drivers of Mercedes-Benz cars in Saudi Arabia are acutely aware of the importance of the Al Juffali family. They have the regional rights to the marque. EA Juffali Brothers, the holding company, sits astride a vast array of local businesses and international joint ventures. The company has grown as Saudi Arabia has but has constantly strived to diversify into other areas through partnerships with the likes of Siemens, Ericsson, Dow Chemicals and DuPont. Its relationship with IBM has placed it as a leader of technology development in the region which gives it an important position in terms of the reforms that are unfolding in Saudi Arabia.

Abdul Latif Jameel Group

This conglomerate has operations in seven distinct sectors. These are automotive, financing, electronics, media and advertising, software, training and development and hotels. The business is best known for having a joint venture with Toyota for the distribution of the Japanese automotive manufacturer in Saudi Arabia.

Its key figures are still chairman Yousef Abdul Latif Jameel and Mohammed, its president. Each individual is believed to own 28.55 per cent of the holding company. Three other family members – Hadia, Hayat and Najia – are believed to own 14.3 per cent each. This is a classic example of the need to prepare for succession issues in times to come.

Oman

Zubair Corporation

The Oman-based group has diversified interests across the globe. Its relationships with Peugeot Citroen and DaimlerChrysler ensure that Oman's roads are peppered with symbols of its wealth. But there are a range of other interests and a developing investments arm that has historically backed the likes of Carlyle Group and Investcorp.

Qatar

Al Fardan Group

The Qatar family traces its business history back more than 100 years. Its founder was Ibrahim, a pearl trader, who operated during the end of the 19th Century. He was fortunate to be based at the Arabian Gulf, blessed with some of the world's best pearls. However it was Hussain Al Farden who really drove the development of the business, beginning with a single jewellery store and currency exchange operation in Qatar. His three sons, Ali, Fahad and Omar then entered the business and drove its diversification strategy into automobiles, exchanges and trading and real estate. Today its most profile assets are its rights to market Rolls Royce and Ferrari cars in Qatar, which given the expected boom from natural gas revenues, should see a rapid development in the growth of this business.

Al Faisal Holding

One of Qatar's leading businesses, this holding company accounts for a group of 30 companies. A third of these – such as Gulf English Schools and the City Center Doha – are 100 per cent owned by the family, but an increasing number are a blend of majority and material stakes in other ventures.

The business began modestly in 1964 – launched as the Gettco Trading Unit – as an automobile parts business set up to service the increasing number of vehicles that were being bought and used in the region.

UAE Abu Dhabi

Al Fahim Group

One of the truly great examples of desert capitalists, the Al Fahim Group has been building a regional business since 1954. Founded by the late Abdul Jalil Al Fahim, it has evolved into one of the largest family groups in the UAE. What began as a single shop in the Al Ain market is now a billion dollar enterprise. It has been able to leverage its position as a leading vendor of luxury cars in the UAE and develop a range of other business lines. Recently it moved into financial services with the launch of Bahrain's International Investment Bank in 2003.

The relationship it has with Mercedes-Benz has been a core factor in its growth. Its relationship goes back to 1962 when it was granted the licence to sell the vehicles in Abu Dhabi. From this it has developed into other areas, such as hospitality, and it owns the Crowne Plaza franchise in the region as well as a range of other assets.

Al Jaber Group

It is no surprise that Al Jaber is receiving an increasing amount of media coverage. For it is in the process of building a 40-floor hotel and office block in the centre of Dubai's Media City. The Media One project will be completed by March 2007. Meanwhile, it is also in the process of building another commercial office block – this time an 80-floor special in Doha – in partnership with the Al Habtoor family.

These projects are just one fragment of a sprawling empire that straddles a range of sectors. The business remains resolutely controlled by Obeid Khalifa Al Jaber, who retains a 100 per cent stake in the rapidly developing empire. According to its somewhat dated website it is built across a construction, industrial and trading triangle. With no financial details available, one can only go on hearsay that it is potentially the largest single family business in the UAE.

UAE Dubai

Al Futtaim

Established in the 1930s, the Al Futtaim Group initially operated as a trading enterprise. Rapid development throughout the 1940s and 50s saw it establish itself as an integrated commercial, industrial and services organisation and reach more than 40 companies in the Al-Futtaim empire. The group was split up a few years ago by the founders Majid and Abdullah Al Futtaim, and each started his own offshoot. MAF Group (Majid) owns the prestigious "City Centers" that can be found in most cities in the region, as well as the hugely profitable Carrefour business; whilst Abdullah retained Toys R Us, Marks & Spencer, Hertz and the new development of Dubai Festival City – a deluxe waterfront development offering a mix of entertainment, dining, shopping, a marina, hotels, residential and office space. Certain businesses continue to be under common ownership such as the lucrative franchise of Toyota and other companies in electronics, retail, jewellery, travel, construction, engineering, marketing communications, logistics, insurance and real estate.

Al Ghurair Group

Saif Ahmad Al Ghurair is the pioneering founder of this UAE business. Today it is famous for owning and operating the Burjuman and Reef shopping malls which have becomes cradles of consumerism, for which Dubai and the UAE is famous. It plays home to retail brands such as Louis Vuitton, Dior and Salvatore Ferragamo. Behind the fashion shoots and glamour lie some more mundane but profitable businesses within the group. For instance, it owns a series of packaging companies and an aluminium extrusions business. Meanwhile there is another branch of the family, headed by Abdullah Ahmed Al Ghurair, the younger brother of Saif, who is particularly famous for launching the Mashreqbank and the Al Ghurair Centre. Collectively, the family controls assets that employ more than 5,000 employees.

Egypt

The Sawiris Brothers

When Onsi Sawiris set up an Egyptian construction firm in 1950 he could not have forseen the giant his sons would take on and create. Orascom Telecom, Orascom Construction and Orascom Hotels and Development collectively account for more than a third of the value of the Egyptian stock market. Consequently the Sawiris family that owns a large slice of them and leads them are Egypt's leading business group.

Naguib, the eldest brother runs the telecoms business; Samih runs hotels and Nassef, the youngest, runs construction. The construction business has become one of the world's top 15 cement producers, manufacturing in excess of 12m tones per year.

During 2005 Naguib Sawiris successfully took control of Wind, the third largest mobile phone operator in Italy, which is expected to float later this year in Milan. It will be keenly watched as an example of how international markets can work without the heavy hand of national protectionism invading the debate. This is especially so given that Weather, the vehicle used to acquire Wind, also controls a 50 per cent stake in Orascom Telecom.

Kuwait

Al Kharafi Group

Nasser Al Kharafi, scion of the family, holds a regional and international influence that stretches far beyond the boardroom. Recently listed as the Most Powerful Arab in the world according to Arabian Business magazine, he has an increasingly large role to play.

His power base is still the business that controls the regional franchises for KFC, Cadbury's and Pizza Hut, amongst others. His business interests span a range of sectors, including a double-digit stake in the National Bank of Kuwait and a partnership with Haliburton of the United States on an Iraq-related contract.

His brother is Speaker of the Kuwaiti Parliament and his sister is president of Kuwait University.

The family's holding company is the Mohamed Abdulmohsin Al-Kharafi Group, which remains one of the largest conglomerates in the region. With a history dating back to the beginnings of the 20th Century, the group is diversified across a range of sectors, including its Americana food brands group, investment, trading, aviation, contracting and manufacturing. Collectively, the business has sales exceeding $4bn.

Bahrain

Yousuf bin Ahmad Kanoo Group

The Kanoo Group is the oldest and largest shipping agency in the Gulf, handling over 5,000 ships every year from Suez to India. The business has more than 10,000 employees and assets of well over $3 billion. Abdulla is head of the Bahrain-based clan, overseeing an operation that stretches from construction and property to travel. The house of Kanoo was founded in 1890 by 22-year-old Haji Yusuf bin Ahmed Kanoo. He began by hiring small boats that would trade foods from India and Africa. Over time it seemed sensible to expand into pearling. His business went into Saudi Arabia in the early 1930s and by the early 1960s, the Kanoo family had expanded into Abu Dhabi, Dubai and Sharjah.

Today, the Kanoo Group is a multi-million dollar operation whose activities include shipping, commercial trading, oil and gas, business centres, insurance and travel agencies. The group has held its own in the face of fierce competition and continues to nurture the 13 trading units that it oversees.

Sixth-generation family members run the business today. Within the family there are a number of outspoken individuals – including modernist author, Khalid Kanoo, and next generation Mishal Kanoo who produces a regular website column focusing on his musings – that are modernisers.

Jordan/Palestine

The Masri Brothers

The Masri family – led by Munib Masri – has been dubbed Palestine's patriarch for many years. Munib, a US educated geologist by training, went on to lead the massive EDGO Group, subsequently helping to create The Palestine Development and Investment Company (PADICO), which has invested $500 million in the Palestinian territories and created 7,500 new jobs. Masri has been dubbed the Palestinian Rockefeller and regularly calls on his fellow tycoons and business leaders to invest directly in Palestine in a bid to develop its economy.

Launched by Masri following the 1993 Oslo Summit, PADICO is a fine example of how investment-orientated economics can provide direct benefit to the State and fuel hope.

Lebanon

The Hariri Family (Saudi Oger)

The Hariri family has a fortune that is often valued at about 25 per cent of Lebanon's GDP. It is a significant amount of capital but has been built brilliantly off the back of a relationship with the Saudi government during the past three decades.

Today the Saudi Oger Group, which is the holding company for the Al Hariri interests, spans a diversified range of businesses. These include telecoms, construction and printing.

There are very few individuals who have been able to simultaneously build great business and political careers, but Rafik Al Hariri was an exception to this rule, before he was assassinated in 2005.

Chapter 4

The Middle East private equity landscape today

RACING AHEAD OF ITSELF

The time is closer to one in the morning than midnight. Arif Naqvi is set to demolish another bowl of wasabi-coated nuts in his Dubai home before beginning to explain the Abraaj story. "The only reason we have raised our $500 million new fund in record time is because we have an excellent track record and operate to global standards." Naqvi is set to spend the next two hours talking through his passion for this industry.

The fourth floor apartment of Yasser El Mallawany in Cairo overlooks the Nile and he gazes upon it. "There are some incredible business opportunities in Egypt. We want to back the smartest companies and help them consolidate their industries, building up champions of Egyptian business."

He is not alone. For every established operator there are scores of others who clamour to join them at the table. Khaldoon Tabaza, the one-time medical student turned reporter cum investor says: "I only have a short time to speak. I am trying to raise my $100m Zad Capital fund and have six meetings to get through this afternoon," before dashing into Riyadh's famous *Al Faisaliah* hotel.

Once these three and the legions of others who are undertaking similar lives pause for breath they will look back at 2005 and 2006 as the dawn of professional private equity investing in the Middle East. Subscribers to *Zawya*, the business news service, who read its Private Equity Monitor will have witnessed the daily emergence of new funds amidst nearly 30 companies that are vying to compete regionally in this space.

So many are announced and never raised. But that is what happens in any boom, when optimism clouds out realism. Students of American economics history highlight the number of railroad companies that would raise money at the outset of the boom. How many are left today?

This is symptomatic of the growth of private equity as an asset class in the region. Every day there is news of a fresh venture being launched to grab the initiative. The latest one is the first new bank to be launched that promises to focus on promoting venture capital in the region. Yesterday, it was a sector-specific oil fund. Tomorrow it will be something else.

Behind the headlines an ineluctable truth is emerging. Private equity as defined by the Western world is evolving and strengthening its position in the region. There may be huge doubt about the availability of deal opportunities here – for there are always many more fundraising announcements than investment ones – but it is an industry that is surging ahead.

And the crowded market is becoming ever busier – the Americans are coming! As this book goes to press the rumours in the region are not of whether, but when, the likes of Carlyle Group and Blackstone will officially announce their intentions to launch funds in the region. In times gone by, both groups, along with so many other traditional Western funds, have

een the region as an ATM machine that provides them with funding. But it now seems as
f they are ready to come to the region and bring their world class approach to bear. This is
ot to patronise the existing operators, many of whom have extensive experience and operate
o high standards. However it will be a striking development for the region that indicates the
ransition from emerging to emerged.

)btaining truly accurate figures about the size of the market is difficult. Banks such as
amba in Saudi Arabia conduct their own private research, but there is no centralised
eceptacle for it.

according to Zawya, new funds under management are believed to have more than doubled
o $5.6bn, however subscribers to its service see pronouncements of new funds being raised
n a daily basis. Previously the pace of growth was significantly less. Prior to 2005 no funds
xceeded $150 million, with the majority of funds being below $100 million. The median size
f a fund is rising as the institutional appetite to invest in the region grows.

his dramatic growth has set the tone for the industry and during 2005 the appetite for
undraising also clearly increased markedly with pronouncements from private equity
ractitioners of plans that will see the industry raise circa $5 billion during the next twelve
onths. It must be recognised that a number of these funds will become phantoms and fail to
aise their money. Yet even if it takes a significantly longer period of time to raise the money
an many expect, there will undoubtedly be a quantum increase in the number of funds
aised in the final quarter of 2005 and throughout 2006.

s might be expected, there is an emerging set of regional brand leaders that have set the pace
y closing significant funds already, led by Abraaj Capital. However, other "mega" Middle
astern funds have emerged, including Jordan Dubai Capital's $272 million fund, and Amwal
l Khaleej's $267 million buyout fund.

hese figures represent only a fraction of the investment set aside to put into private
ompanies from the Middle East. There are a range of other investment groups – such as
)ubai International Capital and Istithmar – which present themselves as private equity firms
ut do not actually raise funds from traditional limited partners.

hey have clients or relationships with existing high net worth individuals or institutions,
o do not go through the process of creating fund structures as a group like Abraaj does.
Jltimately they are all going to compete for the same assets so it is appropriate to compare,
ut they must be distinguished as individual investment vehicles.

Sehind the numbers, other trends can be detected that suggest the growth rates for private
quity will continue to expand. Technology funds are quickly losing attractiveness, while
nergy funds are gaining momentum with $465 million in the process of being closed across
he industry. EFG Hermes, for instance, is planning to launch a brace of specialist sector
unds including one for the oil & gas industry during 2006 and 2007.

Even other specialist international investors are examining plans to launch regional funds. US based Ascent Group, for example, has announced plans to launch a $100 million Ascent Medical Technology Fund that will invest in medical technology equipment businesses throughout the Middle East. Its cornerstone investor will be International Finance Corporation, part of the World Bank, which backs emerging markets.

Peggy Farley, a general partner of the fund, says: "In the United States, a high proportion of GDP has historically gone towards financing entrepreneurs, physicians, engineers and start-up companies, and we will bring this expertise – and best practice framework – to replicate this success in the Middle East."

It is perfectly natural within the context of an emerging market for some funds to attempt to distinguish themselves through sector specialisation. But even when they do this, the majority aim to keep their mandate as flexible as possible, to ensure they do not miss out on any potential opportunities.

Another shift is in the geographic focus of the funds. Prior to 2005, many funds were chasing opportunities in Levant and Egypt. Today, the GCC, with its buoyant economies, is the focus of close to half of the funds being raised. Private equity is also being fuelled by the significant volumes of repatriated capital in the GCC region. Whilst few firm figures are available, it is estimated that somewhere in the range of $10-$15 billion has returned to the region. And this is only the tip of the iceberg – Arab wealth invested outside the region is estimated to be over $1.3 trillion.

Anecdotal evidence suggests that capital in the $50-$70 billion range has also been committed to long-term development projects (in Kuwait and the UAE in particular). Another $15 billion of repatriated capital is expected by 2007. As the GCC continues to evolve, develop and prosper, there will be a growing role for private equity.

Many fear that the profusion of excited investors are not all smart. Abdulmohsen Al-Touq is a long-term investor in many funds, both internationally and regionally, and says, "There are people who are running ahead of themselves. They think they can raise the money. Maybe they can. They think there are endless great deals. I am less convinced. Sometimes it can be smarter to go slower."

Within an increasingly crowded market filled with a number of busy fools as well as shrewd investors, who is driving the industry forward? Who is best placed to capture the opportunities on offer?

THE ABRAAJ JOURNEY

Ask anybody in the Middle Eastern financial markets who is the leading private equity practitioner today and the answer is the ubiquitous Arif Naqvi, founder of Abraaj Capital. Today Abraaj has in excess of $1 billion of funds under management, sourced from a series of regional and international investors who have been impressed by its ability to source deals and exit successfully.

A financial revolution is currently enveloping the Gulf – and Abraaj Capital is its vanguard. This may be luck or exceptional judgement on the part of Arif Naqvi, but his timing of the launch of a classic private equity business principally focused on opportunities in the Gulf has been exemplary.

A confluence of factors – the repatriation of capital to the Middle East following September 11 2001; high oil prices that fuel the demands of China's domestic economy and the impact of globalisation for the great Arab trading families – have all combined to create the perfect environment for private equity in the region.

The business has secured its reputation in the business history of the region from its investments in Inchcape's Middle East assets and Aramex. However, the spirit of the organisation demands that progress continues and Abraaj is facing ever greater challenges to its position in the region. As new funds launch it will increase the competition in terms of securing the best deals and people. Abraaj – perhaps the only brand in private equity in the region at the moment – must continue to sustain its regional position whilst exploiting other opportunities in the Middle East, North Africa and the South Asian region.

Ultimately its success is down to a rounded ability to source and execute transactions. It is a range of factors that begins with an ability to take a macro overview on emerging sectors, source investment opportunities, negotiate a deal successfully, improve its operational performance and then earn a great financial return by exiting effectively. The latest high-profile Abraaj example is the sale of Aramex, the pan-Arab logistics company profiled later in this chapter.

Abraaj is one of a small handful of funds – others include HSBC Private Equity Middle East and Shuaa Partners – that is structured along traditional private equity lines. But it remains the leader by a long way in the region with a 20% market share of the structured funds raised in the region according to the Zawya estimates. This means raising a fund with limited partners investing rather than raising funds on a deal-by-deal basis. These funds then focus on sourcing deal flow, completing transactions, boosting the value of the companies during their holding and then exiting for a significant profit.

Naqvi, the Karachi-born, London School of Economics-educated financier dismisses suggestions that he has become an icon for aspiring investors in the region. However, getting to meet him involves competing for diary time with some very serious business names. When a meeting is finally arranged, it is at his home at 10pm. His story is representative of many financiers in the UAE today, who have made the entrepôt their home from home.

"I studied at Karachi Grammar School, and then got a place to study law at Cambridge. I went, but hated the formality of it and missed my friends who were at the London School of Economics, one of whom is now my wife, and having fun. I persuaded the LSE to take me on but they only had one place left in my faculty, so I went to study the economics of Soviet Russia."

The irony is not lost on this captain of regional capitalism. However, he was never unduly influenced by Stalin's five-year plans. Following graduation he went down the classic route of earning a formal financial qualification, spending four years at Arthur Andersen where he began to develop his outlook and philosophy on business, before moving on to join the Olayan Group.

The four years he spent there played a fundamental part in Naqvi's development. As outlined in the previous chapter, the Olayan Group is arguably the leading trading family business in the Middle East. "So many look up to GE in the United States for leadership and execution skills. I felt the same way about the Olayan Group. It was run well, attracts interesting people and has a modern outlook on how business is evolving."

"Olayan taught me to think for myself, be willing to take thought-through risks and recognise the role that business can play in the fabric of society," says Naqvi. The period of time that he spent at Olayan coincided with the first Gulf War and the business was able to seize on some re-construction opportunities. Throughout these four years Naqvi refined his business thinking and became more determined to set out and develop his own company.

He left in 1994 with a determination if not a business plan. "I thought I could open an advisory business in Dubai, earn enough fees from transactions to keep me going and see what else would emerge." This is the typical outlook of so many entrepreneurs – they have a sense of what they might do rather than a detailed understanding of what it is. His family was uprooted, a base was found in Dubai and Naqvi began the journey that would ultimately lead to the creation of Abraaj Capital.

On arrival, he set up an off-the-shelf company called Cupola as his vehicle. "I was presented with a list by the lawyer. I liked its name. The first fee I earned was for a duty-free kiosk business. I raised money – $8m from six visits – for an $800,000 fee. That $800,000 provided the seed capital for Cupola."

Naqvi realised that he had the skills to earn a very good living as an adviser and could always do that if necessary but his passion was to see if he could build up an operating company. He was influenced by the great trading families who had built their businesses on owning international franchises. So he set about the process of trying to win the regional rights to launch various consumer concepts.

"At Olayan, I could phone anybody and they would take my call. Now, half the people I called would not reply," he says. This will come as no surprise to anyone who has ever tried to launch a start up. Persistence paid off, though, and Naqvi eventually won his first franchise in the form of Color4Kids, a children's furniture franchise that was eventually sold on to a Saudi Arabian firm for $350,000.

"Punching well above my weight, I got TGI Friday's, Pizza Express, Estee Lauder, Thomas Cook, and AlphaGraphics which are all franchises," he says. "I got them all but all needed capital to develop." Naqvi was constantly in the process of raising funds, developing new leads and relying on a core team of people to run the operational business units.

He recognised throughout this period of time that he was always hoping for the transformational transaction. That came in the form of a business being sold by Inchcape, a successful trading company that had developed out of the British Empire. The business had become non-core and Inchcape had appointed investment bank Schroders to sell it.

Commentators expected the local partners, who were significant stakeholders, to win control, but in an exceptionally dramatic process, backed by ANZ Bank of Australia, Cupola won through. It was an incredibly leveraged transaction, with Cupola only utilizing $5 million in an acquisition of over $105 million. Cupola was then re-organised to incorporate the new assets with the intention of developing into a major regional trading business.

This ambition proved very difficult to fulfil. Many of the businesses acquired from Inchcape were reliant on local trading partners, who had come second to Cupola in acquiring the business. Consequently they were not keen on working with Cupola. The impasse was eventually resolved with Cupola selling out a few of the operating businesses it had acquired to various former trading partners, but also as a result, within a 12-month period after the acquisition, repaying all the debt on the transaction. So, instead of becoming a leading trading company, Cupola embarked on a series of these disposals, most of which generated huge returns for the business.

"That process continued and we worked our way through the portfolio," says Waqar Siddique, the former managing director of Cupola, who is today focused on portfolio management at Abraaj. "We then reached the next key moment when we had to do something. We had substantial assets and were questioning what was the best next step and structure for us."

Naqvi hired McKinsey to examine its structure and it concluded that this was a private equity firm masquerading as an operating company. A decision was made to take the investment arm out, leaving Cupola as an operating company with a number of assets. An investment business was founded which became a forerunner to today's Abraaj Capital, formally established in January 2002.

Abraaj Capital's operation, based in the imposing Emirates Towers building in the heart of Dubai, has emerged during its first four years of operation as the key force in the regional industry and some of its landmark investments – Aramex, Jordan Aircraft Maintenance Company, Arabtech, Maktoob and Spinneys have become regional case studies in execution. But it is its ability to successfully raise and invest funds that is becoming a key distinguishing feature.

These funds have been composed of the first and second Abraaj Buyout Funds, a series of Special Opportunities Funds and a Real Estate Fund. Recent newspaper speculation suggests it will also do a joint venture on a $1 billion telecoms sector fund as well in 2006.

Looking forward, its chief challenge is to maintain a leadership position in a competitive marketplace, which is never easy. How Abraaj responds to the challenge will determine whether it can develop into a long-term institution or remains an umbrella organisation for a series of driven personalities.

"The chief challenge is to source deals effectively, manage the portfolio effectively and achieve great returns through our exits for our investors," says Shirish Saraf, Managing Director at Abraaj Capital.

Its structure explains how it is confronting these key issues. It has three central funds – the main holding through which it invests: a traditional buy-out fund; a special opportunities fund; and a real estate fund at any given time in the investment cycle. Whereas the buyout fund is focused on traditional private equity deals, the special situations capital is primarily focused on equity investments in listed GCC companies and pre-IPO situations.

In terms of how the business is internally managed, it has undergone some reorganisation recently. Arif Naqvi remains very much the proactive head of the business; he has appointed a number of key individuals to oversee different parts of the process.

Consequently Shirish Saraf, a Managing Director and co-founder of the firm, who has exceptional skills in raising funds and managing key relationships. He has responsibility for the group's syndication and capital markets businesses. Waqar Siddique, who worked closely with Naqvi in his former days at Cupola has come into the business to boost its portfolio management skills. In the classic tradition of a business that is growing quickly and aware of the need to manage the growth, it has developed a strong finance function under Simon Davies. The latest hire at Director level is Fred Sicre, who has joined from the World Economic Forum, with a wide brief that straddles investor relations, marketing and maintaining the group's position as the industry's and region's thought leader.

Abraaj also has strong connections with a number of the leading trading families throughout the UAE and further afield in the Middle East through its experienced board of directors. The nine individuals include some of the leading industrialists of the region, such as Sheikh Abdulrahman Ali Al Turki, chairman and chief executive of ATCO Group in Saudi Arabia. His extensive list of external directorships includes Investcorp, the Bahrain Investment Group, and Saudi International Petroleum. The Vice Chairman is Hussain Nowais of Emirates Holdings, one of the most respected business leaders in Abu Dhabi, and seven other business leaders carefully selected from around the region. These individuals can open any door they want and this has been a key competitive advantage for Abraaj Capital in recent years. Deutsche Bank is also a shareholder in the firm.

So how is Abraaj focusing on winning the best deals? Fred Sicre says: "This is approached on multiple levels. At the top-down level, all directors have our own individual networks that attract deal flow. A key strength at Abraaj is the quality of the Board Members and how well integrated the Board is in its operations. There are also very strong links to advisers such as

Ernst & Young and KPMG."

However the company has also invested heavily in its bottom-up, research-led approach. The website lists 20 other people who are part of the team involved in sourcing, executing and managing deals. "This team is tracking individuals and industries," says Waqar Siddique. "There is a massive boom and we are tracking who will benefit. For instance, the construction boom will lead to the emergence of specialist employment agencies and low-cost housing companies. We need a deep team of people to give ourselves a competitive advantage."

Part of the success at Abraaj comes down to this triangular structure. Board Members and senior management are feeding intelligence and deal flow to an executive management team that is able to make use of a large research function.

This infrastructure means that there is the manpower to ensure deals that get done are completed effectively. But the sheer number of opportunities under review allows for a patient approach to be taken.

It can easily take more than a year before a vendor becomes comfortable with the concept of selling. Time is spent on the valuation process as so many people do not understand how to value a business. We facilitate the whole of this process, guiding vendors through it, in search of a suitable solution," says Saraf.

Abraaj, which is focused on investing across the whole of the Gulf, Levant and as Far East as India, believes that the principal source of deals over the next three to five years will be family groups and expatriates looking to sell. "After 20 years of working their hearts out, they either want to go back home to Karachi or Surbiton," says Naqvi in his typical down-to-earth style.

Abraaj is also investing a lot of time in building deeper political bridges to the ruling families. The appointment of Sicre underlines this. His connections at the World Economic Forum are excellent and will further assist the group in its bid to get closer to the ruling families and leaders throughout the Middle East. This will give Abraaj an opportunity to get involved in privatisations.

The process of privatisations will be very different to sourcing deals from expatriates," says Sicre. There is a standard approach in the process, but the art of the deal remains keenly important. There are always different elements. To a very large extent, we look at country risk, industry risk and company risk and are well-positioned to get involved if the opportunity presents itself."

Naqvi describes it slightly differently. "The essence of Abraaj is how we build relationships. These bonds have been built up over the past 15-20 years and the nurturing of relationships builds trust. And with trust comes deals. However competitive this region gets, few individuals have invested as much time as we have in building our relationships."

Naqvi and his team are confident about the future role for private equity. "It can play a key role for all sides in the transition to the capital markets," says Naqvi, who today oversees a business that has over $1 billion of funds under management, but appears to be racing towards doubling that number within this year.

This is behind the latest announcement by Abraaj to raise a new $250 million fund, through a joint venture with Sabre Capital to focus on opportunities in India and a similar sized fund partnered with BMA Capital in Pakistan. Saudi Arabia, Qatar and Egypt are also close on the horizon for country initiatives to be launched.

The business is also in a process of institutionalising itself. This is evidenced by its registration with the Dubai Financial Services Authority to operate out of the Dubai International Financial Centre (DIFC). Abraaj, an active proponent of corporate governance in the region, sees this development as just another step in its evolution.

However, is it ready for the challenges that are set to envelop the region? The business is working very hard to become much more than Arif Naqvi Inc. The wish to constantly raise the gene pool is an underlying theme at Abraaj. Today it has a team of more than 80 people who are working on deal origination, transactions and post-acquisition elements to the investment cycle. Its team includes a number of proprietary researchers working inside the business, focused on producing leads that will enable the business to source its own deal flow.

This is exactly what has happened in the ultra-competitive US and UK markets, where deal origination, sector expertise and use of research have become key tools in how funds distinguish themselves.

The sheer quality of Abraaj thinking, as demonstrated by its willingness to publicly distribute its internal research, has contributed to its reputation throughout the Middle East. Over time, rivals will follow its approach and there will be a need to evolve the Abraaj brand innovatively if it is to stay one step ahead. Although Abraaj has become known internationally because of its focus on international best practice, ultimately, it is the deals that get done that will become the basis of the next stage in the development of Abraaj. If the team remains determined and willing to adapt to changing times, the firm will remain in pole position and continue to lead the development of private equity in the region However, it does not have the market to itself.

THE ULTIMATE PRIVATE EQUITY ENGINE

When Sameer Al Ansari, chief executive of Dubai International Capital, speaks, people listen. He is the private equity representative for Sheikh Mohammed bin Rashid Al-Maktoum, the leader of Dubai, and is credited with bringing a new dimension to the asset class in the region.

Dubai International Capital is the private equity arm of Dubai Holding, the parent company and vehicle by which Sheikh Mohammed oversees much of the Emirate's commercial enterprises. Famous for its recent investments in DaimlerChrysler and Tussauds Group, it is also the vehicle through which the ruling family of Dubai invests in international funds. The likes of Carlyle, KKR and 3i have all received investments from DIC in the traditional manner of a Gulf investor. But those times are changing. "There used to be a time when private equity solely meant investing in US and European funds but those days are over," says Al Ansari. Born in Kuwait, he qualified as an accountant at BDO Stoy Hayward and helped launch Ernst & Young in Dubai before leaving to set up his own management consultancy business, Executive Consultants for three years. He then became group financial officer for the Executive Office of His Highness Sheikh Mohammed Bin Rashid Al Maktoum.

So why does His Highness feel the need to operate a private equity firm as well as everything else he owns?

"Critics argue that Dubai Holding is themed real estate," says Al Ansari. "But the reality is that we do lots of different things in different sectors. The philosophy behind Dubai International Capital is to diversify assets away from real estate and Dubai and simultaneously generate above average returns."

In theory, this is the ultimate private equity engine, which is only just beginning to rev up. By combining the investment clout of a State backed captive with an excellent management team, DIC is set to join the ranks of Tamasek and ADIA as one of the largest global investors and if the resolve of its CEO is anything to go by, could well emerge as one of the global leaders in the private equity industry. In practice this has meant an investment to take control of Tussauds Group, the international leisure business, a minority shareholding in DaimlerChrysler plus investments in a number of new and existing funds.

However, DIC is much more than just a deal machine. The political imperative behind the launch of DIC is as interesting as the impact it is having on the Middle Eastern private equity landscape. The unit has a mandate to assist in the development of initiatives that would have a material impact on the future of the Emirate. So if Dubai has an ambition – as it does – to become a regional tourist hub and wants to develop Dubailand as its version of Disneyland, the acquisition of Tussauds will ensure it has one of the world's most popular visitor attractions. This is smart. It blends an investment premise that is focused on backing strong core businesses but each deal has a potential by-product benefit for the wider region.

For much of the past century, the region has been built by the confluence of ruling and trading families and their dynamic ability to develop the sand into one of the fastest growing markets of the world. But the launch of DIC in 2004 sent out a strong message to all those operating in the region.

Private equity is a global industry and is based on a borderless outlook on capital and a willingness to buy and sell assets through an economic cycle. This is in marked contrast to the traditional Arab outlook on business that takes a generational outlook and is happy to hold on to companies for decades.

Private equity and all that it stands for has the formal stamp of approval from one of the Middle East's key ruling families and its development is now being interpreted as a contemporary endorsement of the private equity culture. It is one that is likely to lead to a review of many trading family businesses as they examine private equity structures and see if there is any potential value in launching their own iterations

Al Ansari, whose office is in the heart of Dubai's emerging financial district, clutches his Liverpool Football Club mug of tea, and says: "Primarily our focus is on private equity investments that have a strategic fit within the rest of the Dubai Holding group. And they must give us the right financial returns as well."

Private equity firms all spend lots of their marketing budgets on showing how they are able to add value to their holdings. For any company that wants to leverage off the expected growth in the UAE and rest of the Gulf in the coming years, the investment in Tussauds by DIC will have sent a strong message that there is a new international investor on the map.

However, there is much more to DIC than its high profile investment in Tussauds and Daimler Chrysler. Al Ansari explains the group's strategy: "Firstly we are making direct investments as you have seen in Tussauds. DIC will also make investments in private equity funds such as Carlyle, Baring Vostock, KKR and 3i. It is also investing in newly launched Middle Eastern funds to promote the emergence of a private equity fund in the region."

Secondly, DIC is investing in structured listing equities, including DaimlerChrysler. When DIC invested $1 billion for a three per cent stake it attracted a huge amount of coverage. So why did it sign the cheque? Al Ansari says: "The business is the sixth-largest in the world in terms of its sales. It is the number-one manufacturer of trucks and the number-one manufacturer of luxury cars in the world. There is a good value for the UAE in having a strong relationship with the company. We knew problems existed in the company but believed it could be turned round, so we took the stake."

He has also launched a number of regional funds. The first one is a $272m Jordan Dubai Capital fund, targeting opportunities in Jordan. Expect future funds to be developed in the healthcare, travel and tourism funds. At the recently concluded Private Equity Conference in Dubai in March 2006, he announced plans to establish a new $500million infrastructure fund across the Middle East and North African region with HSBC Bank

Dubai International Capital does not have classic investors in the form of limited partners. Instead, it sources its capital from the balance sheet of Dubai Holding. During its first year it invested in transactions with a cumulative value of more than $3 billion. Can it continue at that pace? "Yes we will. But we are under no pressure whatsoever to put the money to work."

Even the private equity vehicle of Sheikh Mohammed recognises it is operating under the rules of the market. Al Ansari says: "Macquarie and other hedge funds will look at the returns that private equity funds get. Their own returns are diminishing and so they are attracted to the higher returns generated in the private equity investor. That is pushing more money in, leading to valuations going up and returns coming down."

The message is clear. Sheikh Mohammed is keen to encourage the development of private equity and is pleased by the emerging number of family holding companies that are restructuring along the lines of private equity firms. "Globalisation is a huge issue for everybody. Increasing competitiveness brings many other issues out. Private equity is the backbone to any economy."

Dubai International Capital is symbolic of how the region's key financial figures view themselves. Sheikh Mohammed understands that private equity can drive employment and innovation. The creation and development of Dubai International Capital is his way of acknowledging the need to support and be seen to support the development of these fledgling funds.

It is a hybrid approach to the structuring and investing in new funds that is beginning to particularly mark out DIC. To date it has launched a specialist market fund, Jordan Dubai Capital to target opportunities in Jordan and is in the process of developing a new fund to bring the Express Holiday Inn brand to the GCC. Whether these initiatives are being undertaken to avoid competing with the generalist Middle Eastern funds is unknown. However, students of the global private equity industry recognise the development of specialist funds that target either key markets or sectors as a natural staging post in the development of the asset class.

Nonetheless, behind the headline-grabbing investments in assets such as DaimlerChrysler and Tussauds, the unit is facing a number of challenges. It is a classic captive operation and so must function within the context of the wider strategy of Dubai Holding. The DIC management are quick to assure everyone they meet that it is they and not the board of Dubai Holding that make the key decisions, yet they arguably protest too much. Anyone keen to do business on a grand scale in Dubai will be keen to have DIC as an investor as it provides a route to one of the most senior figures in the Emirate.

Its legacy is more likely to be the contributory influence it has on the trading families to develop their own private equity-style operations. If it can act as a catalyst in this respect, then it may have a more lasting impact than any single deal can muster.

FROM THE GULF TO LONDON

At a modern hotel in Marble Arch, over 1,000 people are gathered for the 2005 Emerging Markets Private Equity Association annual conference. The event is packed with people who have come here to discuss the key trends in the market place.

The session marks another step forward in the development of EMPEA, which is emerging as one of the most distinguished trade associations in the global private equity arena. Working in tandem with industry-leading media group *Private Equity International*, it has created an exceptional event, drawing in investors, advisers and commentators from all over the world.

As part of the process, they have created a number of discussion groups, focused on individual markets from around the world. Nearly 80 people are crammed into a conclave to hear the discussion about how private equity is changing the Middle East, more than at any of the other roundtables on other areas of the global emerging markets. It is an interesting shift and one whose significance was not lost on the people present that day.

Private equity is on the ascendancy in the region. The likes of Abraaj Capital, DIC and Shuaa may be the ones giving key-note speeches at conferences around the world, but a profusion of firms is emerging. It is ironic that Dubai – nicknamed the mushroom city for its rapid growth – is playing host to a similar mushrooming of the private equity industry. However, there is a need to define just what private equity is, for it is fast resembling the old joke told by economist John Maynard Keynes: 'Ask two economists for an opinion and you will get three back.'

David Price, one of the two heads of HSBC Private Equity Middle East says: "There really is a need to determine what you mean by private equity. It is used as an umbrella term in the region for investments that are really not always private equity in nature."

"What is private equity?" asks Suresh Kumar, chief executive of Emirates Financial Services. "Well, we are in the process of expanding our team, but we view it as pre-IPO financing to companies that are seeking to grow."

Ali Mohammed Juma, chief executive of Vision Investments of Oman, says: "It should be a pooled fund that allows you to invest in a range of companies."

Charles Milner, the newly appointed managing partner for KPMG's Kuwait office takes a more traditional perspective. "The concept of employee-driven buyouts is non-existent in the Middle East."

All of which leads Price of HSBC to say: "You see. Private equity to me means management buyouts, restructurings, pre-IPO financing and expansion capital and it will only mature in terms of its definition as the market grows up."

PRIVATE EQUITY WITHIN THE REGIONAL INVESTMENT BANKS: PERSPECTIVES FROM CAIRO TO DUBAI

Yasser El Mallawany, the co-chairman and chief executive officer of EFG Hermes, is in expansive mood. It is Saturday morning on a public holiday and Cairo is bustling as ever. El Mallawany lives on the fourth floor of a purpose-built apartment building in the centre of the city. He opens the door into a room that provides a huge contrast to the pulsating tunes at street level. Islamic art jostles with period furniture in his crafted living space.

There are no lines between his approach to home life and work life. They are but the same for the man who has made it his personal ambition to "create the Goldman Sachs of the Middle East".

Six hours later and the venue changes to a fifth floor room in downtown Giza, which plays home to the head office of Hassan Heikal, his co-chairman and chief executive at EFG. Heikal sports tracksuit bottoms and Nike trainers and there is an acute sense that everybody must run very fast to keep up with the pair of them. He has so much energy to spare, he spends most of the interview violently shaking his leg.

He smiles when he hears about his colleague's ambition to develop into the Goldman Sachs of the region. "Yes, that is our short-term three-year ambition." Longer term? The emphasis, according to Heikal, is on "managing the growth so we have an outside change of becoming a next generation Barings or Flemings. We want to build something similar for the Arab World, but without Nick Leeson".

The smiles are wide but the ambition is there. These two financiers want to consolidate their position as the largest independent investment bank in the Arab world and grow it into a sustainable franchise. Today the business has a stock market listing in Cairo and London. There are 420 employees, 70 of whom are senior enough to have access to an equity pool of 20 per cent dependent on the performance of the business. Unsurprisingly it is viewed by some banking analysts as a potential takeover target for a global bank that is seeking increased exposure to the Middle East.

So what is the strategy underpinning it? Heikal says: "Our focus is to mediate between the Arab world and business. We want to capture the domestic flows in the Arab world and then focus on trade that goes on between markets."

Heikal is a passionate bull for the regional market. He says: "Do you know that the combined daily trading of the Gulf and Levant is the same as for the whole of South East Asia, twice the size of Latin America and four times the size of Russia's?"

Maybe, but this scale of opportunity can only be realised if it is managed effectively. What this means is that EFG Hermes is undergoing a series of changes as it tries to implement the systems that will give it the springboard to grow further. The chief question occupying the mind of El Mallawany at the moment is, "How does EFG Hermes develop its human talent for its businesses? So the challenge is to find the right people and get them to share the dream."

Although the opportunities are undoubtedly huge, both recognise that they have yet to develop their private equity franchise to a level that matches their ambitions. El Mallawany says: "Private equity is different from our three other business lines. There is enough to be very strong financially. But in private equity you must have entrepreneurship as well as being a good financier."

Consequently its private equity business is undergoing a period of change as it evolves towards becoming a more focused buyout firm with a range of funds dedicated to the Egyptian market. Its managing partner is Hassan Elkhatib, a one-time engineering student at Cairo University, who subsequently studied in California. He has been a career private equity professional and is now faced with his biggest challenge to date: re-model EFG Hermes Private Equity so it can maximise the opportunities facing an emerging Egypt.

Its historic performance has been strong. It launched its first fund – under the Horus brand – nearly a decade ago and that has become the brand it uses for its private equity investments. It launched four individual funds that collectively have generated a rate of return of 22 per cent, according to Hassan El Khatib, the managing partner of the private equity unit.

But the real change has begun to take hold during the past 18 months. In 2005 EFG Hermes raised a LE50million Technology Development Fund in partnership with the Egyptian Ministry of Communications. It also launched Horus II, a $155million buyouts fund. El Khatib says: "Our philosophy with this fund is based on doing a smaller number of larger deals. We will try to do seven to ten deals and look to grow companies in the region."

This is a shift in strategy. Previously the firm was happy to take minority stakes and negotiate change in its portfolio companies. But those times have gone. El Mallawany says: "We want to support portfolio's regional expansion plans." Heikal says: "We have circa $500million under management today. We need to grow that dramatically and will do so by focusing on opportunities in Egypt. The prices in the Gulf are crazy but it is possible to find realistic opportunities here." The manifestation of the plan is now emerging. During 2006 the intention will be to launch a series of sector specific funds. El Khatib is initially going to raise a $45.5million food and agricultural business sector fund whilst El Mallawany has set himself a target of $100million for a pending oil and gas sector specific fund.

The appetite from investors for these new funds seems to be particularly strong. It is a symbol of a rapidly developing investor base with sophisticated tastes that they begin to consider specific sector funds within an emerging market. The fundraising process has only been helped by the vast amount of capital available to be deployed in the Gulf and a firm with the track record and reputation of EFG is in the enviable position of being able to access it. These new funds provide a framework in which it can add to its investing firepower but also serve the purpose of providing another structure to attract talented fund managers and deal doers who can add to the strength in depth at EFG.

El Mallawany recognises that there is a grain of truth in this. "It is true that our investors are fundamentally in the Gulf. Money is so abundant there. Maybe we are slack at not going elsewhere for investors, but with Egypt on the right track and an understanding of what we do, it seems to make sense to continue doing what we do."

There is one further part of the EFG empire that sits inside its private equity arm and could provide an innovative source of new business in times to come. It still holds the management contract for Commercial International Investment Companies, the largest private investment company in Egypt. This business was a conglomerate composed of scores of businesses in various states of repair. Through the restructure of the group, EFG was appointed in 2003 to realise value for its shareholders, and has subsequently completed 75 transactions. A handful of these have been local listings.

The future for its private equity arm will also be boosted by the reforming zeal of the Egyptian government. It is not afraid of privatisations, as demonstrated by the recent listing of Telecom Egypt, and this provides a further layer of reassurance to El Khatib and his team. "The momentum of change is high. Half of the ministers are reformist in nature. Institutions in Egypt are more mature than throughout the rest of the Middle East. Political reform is moving in the right direction. The ruling party today is totally different from a few years ago, and the investment opportunities are getting better all the time."

Another market-leading investment banking brand in the region is Shuaa Capital of Dubai. Shuaa Capital has come a long way since it was originally called the Arabian General Investment Corporation. Today's business is listed on both the Dubai and Kuwait stock markets and blends asset management and investment banking services, with prime brokerage (Shuaa Securities) and private equity (Shuaa Partners). The business has managed to earn huge brand recognition through its ability to develop regional indices which have become industry standard.

For instance, every day a reference is made to the Shuaa Capital Arab Composite index and the business is promoted. Equally its internal research function regularly pumps out its own branded regional equity research and monthly "Insight" which also contributes to its position as one of the pre-eminent institutional financial services brands in the region.

The business was founded in 1979 under its old name. The genesis of today's multi-pronged strategy began in 2000 when it augmented its investment activities to hold a broader range of financial services products.

Shuaa Partners, which became a separate division of Shuaa Capital in 2004, sponsors and manages several funds, the first of which was a $55 million private equity fund, MENAVEST, targeting the Middle East and North Africa markets. This fund was launched in 1998 with Capital Trust and is now fully invested. It also launched a series of single transaction funds series called "Emirates Opportunities". Its latest one is III which raised around $50 million and acquired a stake worth $80 million in Al Ahlia Investment Company in Kuwait.

It also sponsors and manages a $200 million private equity fund, Shuaa Partners Fund I, L.P. which aims to achieve long-term capital appreciation through selected direct equity, debt and/or equity related investment in mature businesses based in GCC, Egypt, Jordan and Lebanon. Private equity is expected to become a key part of the Shuaa business going forward. The firm believes that its proprietary deal flow and internal research capabilities will play a key role in assisting in the development of this business unit.

Iyad Duwaji, chief executive of Shuaa Capital, says: "We have developed something that did not exist before: we have collected information on about 700 Arab listed companies and that's become the engine for our extensive database which allow us to analyse and compare between sectors and companies across the region."

On June 8, 2005 Shuaa Partners closed its first transaction by acquiring a 10 percent stake in Damas LLC, the leading UAE-based jewellery firm. "Our approach is an opportunistic one. Not everyone wants to sell a controlling stake. We are pursuing both minority investments and control-type transactions" says Abe Saad, Managing Director of Shuaa Partners. The strategy is built on expanding Damas' business into Saudi Arabia and beyond.

"The interesting part about private equity in this region is that it is in its infancy, comparable to what it was like in the US 30 years ago," says Saad. "If you look at funds in the region that have outside LPs, there are really only about three funds, including ourselves (Abraaj and HSBC are the other two)" he added.

Iyad Duwaji added: "It's a lot about educating prospective sellers on what private equity is about. The exciting bit is if you can go in with a controlling stake or even a minority, where you can instigate some financial discipline and efficiency, then you are poised to create immediate value". In the longer term, expansion, industry consolidation and arbitrage all create additional value.

He adds: "Deal sourcing remains critical. We have multiple relationships based on personal histories. Our deal flow is proprietary. We have covered the region for 15 years and are focused on the family owned businesses that have now become market leaders and reached a size where they should consider the public markets.

"Everything I see on the ground encourages me. The mega trends are very positive for our business. If there is a cloud on the horizon, it is the 'bubble' that is developing of the real estate and stock markets. Nevertheless, long-term the GCC area is undoubtedly becoming an economic bloc. The foregoing coupled with the greater Arab Free Trade Association which went into effect on January 1, 2005, will increase the amount of intra-country trade and flow of capital, and will lead to another powerful economic block developing. The other trend is the move by the GCC to integrate into the world economy as they join WTO". He concluded by saying "if oil prices remain over $50-a barrel, it is possible that GDP of the GCC will quadruple to $2 trillion by 2030, and would hence become the sixth largest economy after the US, China, EU, Japan and India'

Shuaa would ideally like to invest in controlling stakes via leveraged buyouts, but recognises that this not always possible in the frothy Middle Eastern financial markets of the day. Consequently, the firm recognises that there are a lot of families in the region looking to go public, while some will want to use private equity as a means of getting to the next level or addressing transition from one generation to the next, as part of a streamlining exercise, prior to going public.

The source of deal flow, the time it takes to complete, the role of advisers and the virtues of external support are all key themes that Shuaa is keen to address at the moment. "Investment activity is being sparked by privatisations of many industries, outside the GCC as utilities, telecommunications and airlines," says Duwaji. "The government is pushing this activity, with many multinational investment firms initiating dialogue and wanting to be part of the process."

Deal times can take years sometimes before a family business feels really comfortable to open up to an outside investor. Duwaji says: "We often have to explain the process of private equity and its benefits. But the upside is that you don't yet see the competition for deals that you see in US and Europe. In most case, the owners are looking for solid partners and hence there aren't many opportunities where they are selling outright".

Saad says the intermediaries will play an increasingly important role in the region. "The bigger multinationals are active, the Deloittes and PwCs. You also have the investment banks, like Shuaa Capital, and other advisory firms like The National Investor. But it's the more established companies that are using intermediaries.

"You have to work with the culture. In my experience it has been reasonably positive. It's not as clear-cut as you would see in the West – you have to bring people around slowly, like in a buy-in. When we say bringing in talent it can mean bringing in a local person or even ourselves showing them how to help with operations or introducing them to new suppliers. But then we also come across companies where things are going well and we don't have to shake things up too much".

Duwaji suggests it is the buoyancy of the exit markets and in particular the strong performance of the Middle Eastern stock markets that has prompted many families to think about private equity as a means preparing to go public. At the same time price expectation have risen sharply on the back of higher multiples in the public markets.

Consequently a key question relates to why companies should go public now. One of the reasons to do so is that it provides a source of liquidity for some mid-sized firms or enables them to get some cash to diversify their personal assets. Up until now, many companies have not gone outside to get money – it's a cultural thing. But the new DIFX exchange is much more favourable to family businesses. They can now list by selling as little as 35 per cent, whereas before, listing in Dubai meant ceding control. The stock exchange also opens up access to international investors in the region and in places like Europe.

THE GLOBAL BANK EXPERIENCE: HSBC

The fund – at $118million – may be small today in the changing scheme of the Gulf but its significance is still high. It remains a captive fund of the only truly global bank that has a base in the region. To many banking groups considering their entry or who have recently boosted their presence in the region, HSBC Private Equity Middle East provides a fascinating case study of how business can be done in the region.

If and when Citibank, Bank of America, Royal Bank of Scotland or BNP Paribas launch private equity affiliates in the region, they will look at how HSBC went about it as one way of entering the marketplace.

Today's business owes its genesis to the Bahrain International Bank where David Knights and David Price met. Whilst at BIB, they completed what many believe to be the first ever buyout in the region, of Nico Middle East. This was a ship repair and supply vessel business that was bought by its management, with backing from **BIB**, from its Swedish parent. Over the course of the next five years, the business unit was grown and finally taken private on the Oman Stock Exchange in 1998. Today it has an excellent reputation under the brand Topaz Energy & Marine.

This success prompted the "Two Davids", as they are universally known in the region, to set up a boutique partnership called Redwood in 1998. It provided corporate finance advice and private equity transactions on a deal by deal basis. But in 2001 it was acquired by **HSBC** to become its vehicle for private equity in the region. The head office had determined a strategy to focus on launching private equity in certain emerging markets where there was already a strong **HSBC** banking presence. Consequently it decided to focus its attentions on South America and the Middle East.

Today there are seven people in its team – with an average age of 44 – investing its \$118million fund. It is believed that half of that figure came from third-party investors. David Price says: "What do we mean by private equity? For us it is investing in existing and profitable businesses with smart strategies. That means management buyouts, restructurings, expansion capital and pre-IPO financing. It does not mean real estate and start-ups."

The group is notoriously publicity shy. Although it has completed nine deals in this current fund, there is only publicity on two, its first investment, the Bahrain based specialist furniture manufacturer, Havelock AHI, and an investment in the advertising-led AME Info media business. "At HSBC, we find we can be more effective operating in the background. We are fortunate that we do not need high visibility to generate deal flow. Our focus is to find suitable value propositions. We are an institutional investor with a reputation for being a strong international bank with offices in most countries in the region. We therefore have excellent contacts which combined with our extensive experience in the region can help build businesses," says Price.

The expectation is that **HSBC** Private Equity Middle East will raise a larger fund in 2006 than its current one. Given the current liquidity in the market it could probably raise a fund of \$ 1 billion or so, but the reticence of its managers in their belief that there are not enough suitable deals to go round means a more prudent approach to fund size will be taken.

However, there is undoubtedly greater interest being shown in what they are doing by head office. During May 2005 David Hodgkinson, the chief executive of HSBC Bank Middle East, who has ultimate responsibility for private equity in the region, gave a presentation to the board explaining what the future holds and received encouraging support to continue developing its presence in the region.

CROSSING THE BRIDGE BETWEEN TRADING FAMILIES AND PRIVATE EQUITY

Faisal bin Juma Belhoul represents a bridge between the trading-focused past of the Gulf and today's developing private equity arena. The tall, slim, Western-educated financier is son of the founder of the Belhoul Group of companies.

Belhoul Group commenced operations in Dubai in 1969 with its origin in the medical equipment business. Under the chairmanship of Dr Juma Khalfan Belhoul, the company set up Gulf and World Traders, a single-line trading company with just two employees. Since then the Group has witnessed a meteoric rise to become a multi-diversified, multi-million-turnover conglomerate for its 13 operating companies, with over 2,000 employees of different nationalities.

With a clear vision of providing a vital link between the rapidly growing technological world and the residents of the country, the Group diversified its interests in hospitals, medical equipment, pharmaceutical and veterinary supplies, travel and tours, manufacturing, construction, retail trading and real estate. According to its website, the Group enjoys a formidable reputation as a supplier of high-quality products and excellent after sales service. Its highly trained and professional personnel, excellent field and technical support and stringent quality control ensure total customer satisfaction – the hallmark of any successful business venture.

Frankly there are a number of significantly larger family enterprises, but what marks Belhoul out is the manner in which it has switched its culture towards that of an institutionalized asset management operation. This owes everything to the dynamism of Faisal bin Juma Belhoul. He says: "Regional family businesses are closer to being wealth management companies".

He energetically argues – at any conference where he can get an invitation – that the traditional family groups of the Gulf are private equity institutions in waiting. Today he runs Ithmar Capital, a traditional private equity fund structure, whilst simultaneously remaining on the board of the restructured Belhoul Group.

Ithmar is an Arabic word that translates as the process of fruition. If Belhoul can succeed in boosting the conglomerate by applying asset management and private equity operational tactics, there is every chance that Ithmar will be invited to provide its expertise to some of the 400-plus other family business that are watching his progress with interest. The fruit will, indeed, have ripened.

But what drove his thinking? "The Middle East's investment landscape is undergoing a fundamental shift driven by a host of factors such as changes in family group structures, succession, World Trade Organisation issues and efficient capital allocation," he says.

Family groups are willing to confront challenges posed by succession and by multi-nationals who increasingly want to become active in the region. Historically, most have been happy to have agency or franchise agreements that require low levels of financial commitment and involvement. But as the region develops into a more important market, it is unsurprising that the brands want to take a much more active involvement.

Belhoul recognised these trends were emerging during the mid-1990s and then spent a number of years evolving his thinking to determine the best plan. At its heart the plan was based on shifting the philosophy of the Belhoul family from one of operators to one of investors.

A general assembly was set up including the eight key family members which ensures their interests are represented. At regular intervals they are presented with updated information from a management board, which overlooks a fund management company and includes five elected members of the general assembly and four external advisers. "That board identifies the asset class and allocations we want to invest in and then evaluates the best managers to develop the plan," says Belhoul.

Long-term decisions are then made by the fund manager about the most effective and efficient sectors and investments to be in. The subsidiary management teams are left alone to get on with the managing of those businesses. This is much more closely aligned with the structure and strategy of an asset management firm.

"There is a unique opportunity and challenge for private equity groups in the region," says Belhoul says. "And what role will family groups play? "Family groups are a key source of private equity deal flow because some are seeking to exit non-core, but in many cases profitable businesses, while others are looking for strategic investors for late-stage pre-IPO play or are seeking to consolidate their regional presence in core businesses."

As a result of the restructuring and track record of the Belhoul Group, Faisal Belhoul moved on with other partners and institutions to setup Ithmar Capital as a leading specialized private equity firm focusing on GCC based and related opportunities.

THE EMERGING DEVELOPMENT OF SECTOR-SPECIFIC FUNDS

A sure sign that private equity is developing in a region comes with the development of sector specific funds. It has long been stated in the West that there is probably room for a single-digit number of global mega funds, such as Carlyle and Blackstone, with the great majority working hard to distinguish themselves.

Andrew Hartley, joint head of UK mid-market firm August Equity - which was formerly known as Kleinwort Capital until its March 2006 re-branding - developed a strategy to invest in four key sectors to distinguish itself. So do many others and now this approach is slowly beginning to come to the Middle East as well.

One of the most high-profile sector-specific funds is GCC Energy Fund. Adil Toubia, a Sudanese national who spent 21 years working at Schlumberger, is now its chief executive. He oversees a $300 million fund that was launched in March 2005. Its focus is to make private equity and mezzanine investments into the energy and power sectors in the GCC. This includes upstream, midstream, downstream hydrocarbon sectors, power generation, transmission and distribution sectors. Its ambition is to market itself heavily in these core sub-sectors, be seen as a leader and thus develop a specialist franchise to complete deals. It cannot compete now with the likes of Abraaj, Shuaa and HSBC as a generalist so is focusing on building a specialist franchise.

Toubia says: "The region is not getting the coverage it deserves. There was not enough attention being paid to what is going on when I joined the fund 2 years ago. The idea was launched three years ago. Energy was its focus. No-one has specialised on energy in the Middle East. We are the first sector specialists fund in the region. There are lots in the West, but it is a new concept here."

GCC is the latest fund to be developed by Standard Bank, a specialist emerging markets investment bank. It has partnered with Gulf International Bank (GIB) of Bahrain and Emirates National Oil Company (ENOC) to develop this fund. But will there really be enough deal flow for a specialist fund?

Toubia says: "Deal flow comes from multiple sources: management teams, banks, ENOC and those that approach us directly. The first deal will be before the end of this year." He is tight-lipped on whether his fund hopes to become the vehicle through which a number of trading families with interests in energy access private equity. "Trading families are private equity firms in disguise. Some of them are based on agency style businesses and others have developed into other businesses that require capital. The talent from within these families is the breeding ground for the next generation of private equity leaders in the region and these are exciting times to be in private equity."

PRIVATE EQUITY VS VENTURE CAPITAL IN THE REGION

If, according to Samer Alhaj, an executive vice-president at Kuwait's Gulf Investment House, the state of regional private equity is embryonic, then the state of venture capital is even less well formed. Venture capital is very distinct from its larger sibling, private equity. There may be huge excitement at the potential of investing in the next Google or eBay, but the reality is that 90 per cent of all start-up investments fail. Consequently there is not a huge market for venture capital in this region. Even those involved in it prefer to use the term "development capital" to describe what they do.

Ahmad Mohammad Al-Sari is a co-founder of the Gulf Venture Capital Association, which is vying with the Arabian Venture Capital Association to become the leading trade association in the region. Visitors to his fifth floor office in downtown Riyadh are confronted by lots of images of stallions, which relates to Malaz, the name of his management company. He presents two cards, one for Malaz and one for the GVCA. "To be honest, if you translate directly from the Arabic, it should say the Gulf Daring Capital Association, as there really isn't an Arabic word for venture," he says.

Whereas in the West there are brands such as Kleiner Perkins or Benchmark – which are to the venture industry what Carlyle and Blackstone are to the buyout world – there are no venture equivalents of Abraaj, Shuaa or EFG Hermes in the Arabic region.

However, the market is not dead. There are figures who are dedicating their energies to the development of a technology and venture focused world. For instance, Abdulaziz A Jazzar and Ahmad Mohammad Al Sari are trying to raise a $100 million fund under the ICT Ventures brand. In Jordan there is the Accelerator Fund, whilst IT Ventures in Egypt is bidding to raise another $100 million fund.

They are not alone in terms of individuals who are out there trying to take ownership of this space. Step forward Khaldoon Tabaza, the Jordanian serial entrepreneur who is in the perennial process of attempting to raise a $100 million fund. "It will be called the Zad fund, take three months from now to raise and be somewhere between $50 million and $100 million in size." Or that, at least, is the hope, as he has conducted 70 meetings to get to a stage where a cornerstone investor may now be on the horizon.

Only time will tell if he can actually deliver a fraction of what he promises, but he has boundless energy and a determination to succeed that warrants further investigation. He is a relentless networker and name-dropper. "The World Economic Forum has made me one of their young global leaders. So are the guys from Google and Skype."

The name Zad originates from the name of King Solomon's horse – a legendary stallion called Zad el Rakib. Tabaza has three cornerstone investors in the fund. These are Ntec, the National Technology Enterprises Company of Kuwait, Technology Venture Capital (which is a subsidiary of the Kuwait Investment Authority) and PrimeCorporation, another investment firm.

Tabaza, who originally studied medicine in Jordan, decided against a career in medicine and instead alighted upon the media industry. He launched Arabia Online in 2001. "It was the first Arab start-up to raise venture capital money to the level we did. We raised $25 million from Intel Capital, Compaq, Al Waleed and Shuaa Capital," says Tabaza. Subsequent enterprises included Ideavelopers, the first early-stage Egyptian fund, which was backed by the Egyptian government. To date he has set up a further 12 companies, including online advertising business NetAdvantage. The reality is that a number of them have seen their life support machine turned off, but these experiences have cheerfully prepared him for his next major enterprise, the launch of a $100 million fund.

His next challenge is Riyada Ventures, which is his own personal vehicle and a co-sponsor of the Zad fund. "Riyada will be a private equity, advisory, corporate finance company. It will focus on knowledge-based industries in the MENA region. We hope to raise a minimum of $50 million up to a maximum of $100 million. It will be to invest throughout the region. But we will focus on key countries such as Jordan, Saudi Arabia, Lebanon, Egypt, UAE. It will be the largest venture fund in the region. All the large funds are buyout funds."

The energetic team at Zad – currently composed of three partners and a further three principals, demonstrating a commitment to bring a proper infrastructure to the sourcing and execution of prospective deals – has already highlighted 20 potential transactions.

Riyada Ventures feels that a lot of potential entrepreneurship comes about as a consequence of oil. "It gives us an unfair advantage. Governments leverage the high oil prices and incomes to build infrastructures without taxing – creating attractive work environments that are better than Europe and the US to create jobs throughout MENA. In a way this does mean that the urgency of entrepreneurship is not fully developed in some people."

This view is echoed by Rami Bazzi, a senior investment manager at Injazat Capital. Based in the heart of Dubai's Media City, this group has raised a specialist technology and healthcare fund. He believes that there is an extensive depth of latent talent in the region and is keen to use private equity funding to develop it.

The Beirut-born investor studied in Canada's Montreal before navigating his path to Dubai and assisting in the development of Injazat.

"We take stakes up to 49 per cent levels but do not get involved at an operational level. We feel that we want to be backers of management teams, who are executing their own strategies, rather than feeling a need to get involved in the setting of the strategy," says Bazzi.

He has been an active proponent in arguing for the development of a corporate governance code of conduct for investors in the region. He says: "The role of corporate governance and how we handle it will be key to the development of the Middle Eastern financial markets. There should be a corporate governance code of conduct that codifies the relationship between management and investors, builds transparency."

At the time of writing Injazat was examining plans to list a fund on the UK's junior stock market, AIM, in a bid to generate international interest in the Middle Eastern region. Although the Middle East seems unlikely to be the base of a next generation Google or eBay, there is ample energy which is likely to contribute to the gradual development of a venture capital and seed financing industry.

Governments are likely to do more to support this – it is part of their wider challenge of embarking on initiatives that will satisfy larger employment requirements. Successful self-starting entrepreneurs can play a key role in generating employment and the regional governments will be expected to build stronger links and provide greater support to them over the coming times, which should boost the development of this part of the market in times to come.

THE NEW FIRMS IN THE GAME

Why should a start-up private equity group be classified as a major force? Gulf Capital has worked hard to find a distinguishing business model that is different and warrants closer attention. In December 2005 it unveiled a plan that was based on securing best of breed knowledge from an advisory board that was also a key investor in the firm.

Names such as Suhail Al Mazroui, chairman of Aabar Petroleum Investment Company (Oil & Gas), Khaled Juffali, vice-chairman of E.A. Juffali & Brothers (Industrial) and Dr Ali Dayekh, president of Saudi Group for Construction Materials (Construction) are just three examples of great reputations that add genuine kudos to the group. Previous chapters have touched on the significance of merchant families, such as the Juffalis, and to be able to access this calibre of person adds huge value to the Gulf Capital offering.

It is this collection of individuals that has ensured Dr Karim El Solh has been able to win the funding that he requires to build a presence. He is a determined man and recognises – possibly in a similar vein to Arif Naqvi at Abraaj – the need to generate original thinking in his plan. Hence he has been shrewd enough to hire Imad Ghandour as head of research and strategy. Ghandour is seen as a key figure in the regional market from a research perspective and adds deeper understanding of the market to the team.

However there will be more to Gulf Capital than merely its advisory board. Its operational team is composed of internationally educated people who are modelling themselves on a classic merchant bank. There are currently 20 full-time people on the payroll, which is expected to rise to 50 within 12 months. The essence of the business will be to blend financial engineering skills with a nous for nurturing businesses.

For instance Thomas Fink, the former chairman of Triton Energy in the United States and Waseem Assad, the ex-head of Schlumberger Middle East Services Business, will be full time and focused on investing in and running energy businesses.

As of April 2006 the business had capital of $330million and was structured as a joint stock company that is based out of Abu Dhabi. It has 300 shareholders who will feed it transactions as well as commit to increase their investments subject to performance. Currently the plan is for the business to go public in years to come but it must demonstrate two years of profitability before it can go public.

Another important player in the regional private equity industry that is relatively new is Geneva based Swicorp. Swicorp is a recent entrant to the private equity industry in the Middle East but has a long corporate finance heritage in the region from which to draw down on. The business was launched by Kamel Lazaar in 1986 as a specialist corporate finance boutique for the Middle Eastern region. Lazaar was formerly a vice president at Citibank and decided to launch his own venture.

In its first 20 years the boutique has developed a strong reputation in mergers and acquisitions, privatisations and in offering strategic advice, particularly to multinationals that were keen to break into the Middle Eastern markets. Its credentials in corporate finance are strong. Swicorp advised on the first merger of public companies outside the banking sector in Saudi Arabia, worked on Algeria's first privatisation outside the energy sector as well as most famously advising France's Danone on Laiteries Djurdjura, the Algerian market leader in fresh dairy products.

It has accumulated contacts and transaction expertise that are the foundation blocks of its private equity arm. Now that it has decided to enter the market, it is doing so with a series of initiatives, which are all distinctive and suggestive of a unique approach which is being brought to bear on the region.

For instance, its first fund was **MENA** Water Ventures, which was launched in partnership with Groupe Danone in late 2003. This fund was the first corporate venturing fund to be launched in the Middle East. Groupe Danone gets the opportunity to further understand and develop its Middle Eastern market whilst Swicorp are the management company behind the fund.

It was followed in mid-2005 by Intaj Capital, another example of a corporate backed fund, this time by the Savola Group of Saudi Arabia. Savola is a leading Saudi Arabian business that is family controlled. It had been examining different techniques of developing a private equity business and partnered with Swicorp to launch this fund. Savola is the cornerstone investor in the first round closing of $60million with plans to close the fund in 2006 with $200million.

Its third fund is a departure from its corporate venturing business model. Launched in December 2005, Swicorp Emerge Invest has raised $100million to invest in Iran, Algeria and Sudan. It is positive proof of how investors are willing to back more funds focused on the volatile areas of the Middle East.

These three countries are all likely to face political and economic changes over the coming three years, which are expected to present a blend of corporate finance and private equity opportunities for Swicorp, which has a longstanding track record in all three markets.

And finally, no section on the newer entrants can be complete without a discussion on arguably the most high profile of them all, Istithmar. Is Istithmar a private equity firm in waiting? Had the question been asked in 2003 when the unit was launched, the answer might have been yes. Two years on and the answer is much less clear cut.

Today it has just launched an international campaign to raise its profile through advertisements in *The Economist*. Technically it is part of Dubai World, a holding company of Dubai Ports World, Free Zone Corporation, Nakheel and Dubai Multi Commodities Centre.

During the second half of 2005, Istithmar made two headline grabbing investments in prime real estate locations such as London's One Trafalgar Square and 230 Park Avenue in Manhattan, a 34-storey gold-domed office block which sits at the top of Park Avenue, New York. These latest deals have led many to believe that Istithmar is simply another international real estate investor, leveraging the natural resource wealth of the Gulf to fund its mergers and acquisitions spree.

But go beneath the surface and one finds a business that has a strategy broad enough to encompass real estate, structured debt and private equity deals.

Examples of its disparate taste in transactions includes investing in Hyflux, a Singapore water technology company, and even backing the Wharton Global Family Alliance, which is likely to give Istithmar an edge on research into family businesses. Could it be poised to apply leading edge thinking on how to maximise family businesses, produced by the world's best academics, on behalf of Gulf businesses?

Ultimately Istithmar cannot be compartmentalised. It was originally established by the Ports, Customs and Free Zone Corporation of Dubai in 2003 with capital of $2billion. The original mandate was to build businesses across a number of sectors that would fuel the development of Dubai. These companies would all harness best practice international standards and apply them to the benefit of the UAE. Consequently during its first 12 months it invested across a range of sectors including financial services, manufacturing and healthcare.

However this conglomerate style has been refined during its second year. Today it classifies itself as an investor that is focused on three core principles – ideas, integrity and inquiry – which would not look out of place in the marketing literature of a West Coast venture capitalist outfit.

The high-profile David Jackson, who is a regular commentator at international conferences on the economic dynamism of the region, does project a positive impression. However, the business will need a few more years of investing before it can determine its own reason for existing.

EXTERNAL PERCEPTION: THE GULF VS. THE WIDER MIDDLE EAST

"Come back to me in ten years and let's talk," says a director of one of the world's largest buyout funds. He dismisses the notion of a vibrant industry emerging. However, his viewpoint is less and less common. Less than a decade ago, the international private equity community was of the belief that the Middle East existed as a source of funds and no more.

Today, that perception is changing. Mark Mobius of Templeton Asset Management, who is arguably the greatest living emerging investor on the planet, says he has been monitoring the region closely for a long time. "There are great opportunities for private equity in the region," he enthuses.

Templeton Asset Management has installed a sales team in Dubai, but is currently restrained by limits on investing in other funds. Tim Marsden, global head of Corporate Finance at Norton Rose, believes that it is "only a matter of time until the international players move in". So who is most likely to come first? Carlyle Group? Blackstone? Apax Partners?

Max Burger-Calderon is the chairman of Apax Partners Asia business. Apax has enjoyed a strong history, principally in Western Europe, but is now examining the potential to grow in new markets. "In the 15th century the world was dominated by India, China and the Middle East. Maybe we are going to go back to the future."

Today, Apax still looks at the Gulf as a source of funds rather than as a place to invest directly. Will this change? "The merchant banks are working to convince the governments to privatise some of the entities, so I would assume there is a lot of dialogue going on. This region has a lot of money to invest and is taking an extremely professional approach. If you talk to some of the larger organisations it is like talking to a sophisticated US or UK pension fund. You are sitting across the table from someone who is managing anywhere between $50 billion to $200 billion."

However, like so many investors he distinguishes between the Gulf and much of the rest of the Middle East. "You are not going to invest in unstable markets, but focus on the open ones, like Egypt, Dubai, Lebanon," says Burger-Calderon. This is a view shared by other leading figures in the international private equity arena.

Mario Giannini, chief executive of Hamilton Lane, points out: "It is a very idiosyncratic industry with each region developing differently." Just as the term Western Europe is an umbrella one for a series of different cultures, languages and themes, so too is the term Middle East. There is a need for private equity investors entering the region to develop a strong local presence, build strong links to the political and business elite in any one country and demonstrate a long-term commitment to an area. Only then will they begin to realise the potential of a country, which needs to happen collectively to demonstrate expertise across a region.

The investor relations departments of many US and Western European private equity funds will have a long list of Middle Eastern and Gulf investors or target investors. They will naturally invest time in the region to win over their support. Although figures do not exist to suggest what percentages of Western funds are composed of Gulf capital, the number is considerable.

Those investor relations managers who are tasked with manning the support of existing and potential investors do not keep track of individuals and families in other emerging markets as they do in the Gulf. It has always been a huge source of capital for deals that are done in the United States and Western Europe because the reality is that the Gulf region is unlike any other emerging market.

For a start it has an abundance of indigenous wealth. The Middle East is third behind the United States and Europe as a source of investment capital for international private equity funds seeking investors.

Most senior Western private equity professionals have stories of spending time presenting to Gulf families for investment capital. Andrew Hartley is the joint managing director of August Private Equity, previously Kleinwort Capital, which was the private equity arm of Kleinwort Benson before securing its independence. During that period he undertook a series of flying visits to potential shareholders in the Gulf.

He says: "I remember having a series of meetings with potential investors. Some would have a lot of knowledge about Western financial markets and others gave the impression of following the lead of their advisers. I would then spend all night taking phone calls about the deals we were simultaneously working on. It is an amazing region."

There is much more to the Middle East than just the Gulf. Arguably there is more entrepreneurial depth in the Levant region which is not blessed with the same natural resources that the Gulf enjoys.

Foursan is a firm that has been launched by the Masri cousins of Palestine. It has offices in Jordan and London. Leith Masri, one of its co-founders, says: "Egypt and Tunisia, for instance, have a very active industry that has been overshadowed by the recent interest in the Gulf, where the money is congregating. There are more deals in older Arabia and the Levant, which is not surprising when you consider that the wealth gravitates from the richer countries to the poorer ones. There are more opportunities in less wealthy markets, where families and governments are more prepared to give up assets, there are more privatisations and more companies in need of capital."

Foursan is the manager of the $50m Jordan Fund, with Deutsche Bank also playing a support role on the Fund.

Foursan is also currently launching a regional private equity fund focusing on emerging regional markets such as Libya, Algeria, Sudan, Iraq (once the situation stabilizes) and Jordan/Palestine. He highlights XPress Telecom, a mobile telecoms start up deal in Jordan that has received in excess of $100m funding as a great example of what is achievable when financiers put their mind to it. "A wide range of partners came together in a syndicate. These included Foursan, a Saudi family investment company, and a number of leading Jordanian investors. XPress was also able to secure $65 in debt financing from US Export-Import Bank which would not have come without a high level of transparency, and this is the largest telecom financing that EXIM has done in the Middle East." The business is in the process of merging with a similar operation in Saudi Arabia and will become a regional holding company for various telecommunications assets. Looking forward he believes that some of the next key markets will be Morocco and Libya although there remain a number of question marks over transparency in a number of regional markets.

He says: "The regional market is still maturing. There are many people saying that they want to do private equity deals, but not many approaching it in a private equity manner. There are many undervalued assets and poorly managed companies. But to have the openness that we have seen in the US and, to a lesser extent, Europe, with an investor coming in on the same, or better, terms to existing investors has not been easy for people in the region to accept."

Masri argues that management teams in the region need assistance in terms of governance and business development assistance as well as financial assistance. He says: "We can work with a company in Morocco and introduce them to customers in the Gulf, which is what they need. There is good entrepreneurship and ideas in the region, but management teams are not always strong. Governance is poorer for historical reasons.

The two main ways in which we help create value: through stronger financial controls and advice on business development angles."

However he counters that it is futile to apply a blanket generalization about the state of private equity in the wider Middle East. "The infrastructure is not developed in a private equity sense. The size of the market has significantly increased and that has made it more interesting for local and foreign players, who are now looking at setting up offices in the region. But some countries, led by UAE, Jordan and Egypt are making themselves more attractive for private equity than others who are making less effort."

In fact the region is developing into a more competitive landscape with more funds and investors chasing a smaller number of high-quality deals in the "obvious" markets, but there are several untapped markets, such as Libya, where enormous opportunity exists. Hopes remain high that privatisations, disposals by trading and expatriate families and multinationals will provide a steady source of deal flow to satisfy the various private equity investors, but it will remain the case that leading private equity houses will have to create and develop many of their deals.

CHAPTER FEATURETTE 1

– Key Investor profiles

1. Abraaj Capital

Arif Masood Naqvi is the visionary behind Abraaj Capital. He received a classic training, first at Arthur Andersen and then at the Olayan Group, learning the mechanics of business in the Middle East and the particular importance of building long-term relationships with key individuals who have developed leading trading firms over past decades.

Naqvi represents the essence of private equity in the Middle East. Originally from Karachi in Pakistan, he is an economic migrant, who made a conscientious decision to build a private equity firm from a Dubai base. His involvement with the World Economic Forum suggests that he is keeping open the possibility of jumping into politics. He has the potential to become a senior figure in regional politics.

Shirish Saraf is a flamboyant financier who has been intimately involved in the development of Abraaj since its inception. Saraf is one of the most effective and well connected fundraisers in the Middle East. His ability to win over the support of leading trading families and the depth of his contacts has been a key factor in the ability of Abraaj to scale up its fundraising abilities.

He began his career with Salomon Brothers and BDO Stoy Hayward in London. The two core roles that have led to his reputation as one of the most effective financiers in the region came during his time at TAIB Bank in Bahrain and the subsequent launch and development of Oriel Investment Company in 1998.

Fred Sicre is the newly appointed head of investor relations, marketing and thought leadership at Abraaj Capital. He has more than 16 years' experience in global issues, regional development agendas and community building. He was most recently managing director for the World Economic Forum, prior to joining Abraaj.

As Managing Director at World Economic Forum, he was responsible for all international activities of the organization and led relations with political leaders worldwide. He spearheaded the move of the 2002 Annual Meeting in Davos to New York City as a sign of support to New Yorkers just 4 months after 9/11. In June 2003, he was responsible for the Extraordinary Annual Meeting in Jordan following the Iraqi conflict that brought together 1,200 business and political leaders. He is a strong and accepted voice amongst business and political leaders in the region on issues of reform and economic development.

Sicre has initiated dialogue and reconciliation initiatives during South Africa's transition to democracy and between Palestinians and Israelis. He was responsible for the historical Casablanca summit in 1994 under the patronage of the late King Hassan of Morocco which served as the economic leg to the Oslo peace plan. He also launched the first Africa and Arab World Competitiveness reports and is a founding member of the Arab Business Council. He recently edited South Africa at Ten – a book celebrating the ten years of democracy in the country. His global network of decision makers and vast experience in emerging markets are poised to become a critical asset to the firm.

Waqar Siddique joined Abraaj in September 2005 after a decade working at Cupola, which has developed as the personal investment vehicle of Arif Naqvi, with diverse business interests in consumer, retail, information and engineering sectors in the Middle East and South Asia. At Abraaj his focus will be on portfolio management of the investee companies. Prior to working at Cupola he was the Development Manager in the Group Treasury of Mawarid Holding Company, a leading business conglomerate based in Riyadh.

Simon Davies oversees all of the Abraaj finance function, thus playing a key role in the management of its growth, as well as sitting on the board of JorAMCo, Spinneys and Aramex Holdings. Prior to joining Abraaj, he spent six years as Finance Director at Publicis Groupe UK. He is highly regarded in the region and has played an important role in the development of the Abraaj franchise.

2. Dubai International Capital (DIC)

Sameer Al Ansari is the founding chief executive of Dubai International Capital. Most recently he was group chief financial officer for the Executive Office of His Highness Sheikh Mohammed bin Rashid Al Maktoum. He is a board member on several Dubai Holding companies as well as Dubai International Financial Centre and Dubai Media Inc.

When Dubai Holding, the parent company of DIC, decided that it wanted to develop a classic private equity business it was Al Ansari who was appointed to head it. The Liverpool Football Club supporting investor is now one of the chief private equity professionals in the region.

Kuwaiti-born Al Ansari, a Fellow of the Institute of Chartered Accountants in England & Wales, has a keen understanding of entrepreneurs given his own experiences. He spent three years launching and running Executive Consultants

Alan Hyslop brings UK private experience to DIC. Following graduation from the University of Strathclyde, he qualified as a chartered accountant. His private equity career began in 1994 when he joined 3i, regarded by many as the training ground for those in the European private equity industry, before leaving to join PPM Ventures. PPM has a track record of investing internationally, and became his base before leaving to join DIC. He is tasked with two chief challenges: overseeing the investment by DIC in other private equity funds and sourcing co-investment opportunities.

Sylvain Denis, the head of Direct Investments, has more than 14 years in corporate and investment banking and corporate finance. His most recent experience was his work as finance director of the Executive Office of his Highness Sheikh Mohammed bin Rashid Al Maktoum. His focus inside DIC is to head up its direct investments unit. The first example was the Tussauds Group in a classic leveraged buy-out. He is also credited with contributing to the creation of new companies that are set up to bring international brands to the region. The first example was the creation of the $150million Ishraq investment company, formed to bring the Holiday Inn Express brand of hotels to the region.

3. EFG Hermes Private Equity

Yasser El Mallawany is currently the Chairman and CEO of EFG Hermes and chairman of its private equity unit. The cigar-chomping El Mallawany is credited with being a major player in the development of the financial services industry in Egypt. He began his career in finance with the Commercial International Bank (CIB) in Egypt for 16 years before leaving to lead the development of EFG Hermes Private Equity.

Hassan Heikal is the son of the famous Egyptian author, who chose finance over literature. He is a former Goldman Sachs investment banker who shocked his colleagues in the mid 1990s by deciding to jettison a bright future there to return home and launch the bank. He is seen as exceptionally dynamic within the region and a solid counterweight to El Mallawany.

Hassan El Khatib is the managing partner of EFG Hermes Private Equity. Previously he worked for the Commercial International Investment Company. He gained an MBA from the California State University and is a certified management accountant.

4. Shuaa Partners

Iyad Duwaji is the chief executive of Shuaa Capital, who was appointed in 1995 and is credited with leading the development of the business into a multi-discipline financial services organisation. The Syrian-born, American educated financier was instrumental in the development of Shuaa's private equity portfolio with the launch of the Middle East North Africa Fund in 1998. He is a member of the Arab Business Council and serves on the board of a range of companies across the region and in Europe. He gained his MBA degree in finance from the University of Texas at Arlington.

Abe Saad is managing director of Shuaa Partners private equity arm. He brings broad-based private equity experience of over nine years to the firm, having joined Shuaa from Allied Capital Corporation of the United States. Prior to working at Allied Capital, he held a senior position at Carlyle Group having begun his career as a management consultant at Booz Allen Hamilton. Saad holds a MBA from the MIT Sloan School of Management, and is fluent in Arabic, English, French and German.

5. HSBC
Private Equity Middle East

David Price is the Perth born co-head of the private equity business. He built up extensive experience in the investigation and turnaround of ailing companies in Australia before moving to the UK and developing a corporate finance and venture capital background. He went to Bahrain International Bank to assist the development of its private equity business, where he met his future business partner, David Knights. The duo then left to set up Redwood before it was acquired by HSBC as the basis for its private equity footprint in the region. He has over 15 years experience in managing private equity transactions in both the UK and Middle East.

David Knights is a banker by background. His initial training was with JP Morgan in New York, and he worked for a number of years with Saudi International Bank in London, which was managed by Morgan. He joined Bahrain International Bank to set up its corporate finance business. He has been involved in the structuring of, and investment in, private equity transactions in both Europe and the Middle East for over 17 years.

6. Ithmar

Faisal bin Juma Belhoul is the founder of Ithmar Capital and former CEO of Belhoul Group of companies. He led the process of operational restructuring of the family companies and converting them into more efficient, professional entities. He is a strong advocate of converting family business groups into professional asset management companies.

Khaldoun Haj Hasan was formerly a VP at Abraaj Capital. His expertise is investor relations, capital raising and execution of exit strategies. Between 1996 and 2001 he worked as the partner's asset director of Al-Bawardi Enterprises and group commercial manager of Al Fahim Group of companies, two of the largest family-owned businesses in the GCC.

7. Swicorp

Nabil Triki joined Swicorp in February 2003 and heads Swicorp's private equity activities. Prior to joining Swicorp, Nabil spent several years as a project leader with the Boston Consulting Group in Paris where he led numerous business strategy, corporate development and operational restructuring and organisation assignments for leading international companies, with specific focus on consumer goods & retail, technology & telecom, and industrial goods. Whilst at BCG, Nabil also launched and co-managed a €100million corporate venture capital fund. Prior to post-graduation, Nabil worked as a project manager for Honeywell in Los Angeles and as a senior analyst in corporate development for Unilever in New York. He holds an MBA from the University of Chicago and a Masters in Engineering Science from the Massachusetts Institute of Technology (MIT).

Kamel Lazaar is the urbane founder of Swicorp, who has more than 20 years' experience in international banking and finance. He is the driving force behind the development of Swicorp and is credited with helping it augment its traditional corporate finance product base with a private equity offering as well.

Daniel Schenker runs the group's operations in Saudi Arabia, arguably its most important marketplace. A Swiss national, who is fluent in English and French, Schenker joined Swicorp in 1991 and has played a key role in building its credentials in the marketplace. Key transactions successfully driven by Schenker have included the leveraged buyout of DAC and the joint ventures of Henkel in Saudi Arabia.

8. GCC Energy Fund

Adil Toubia is central to the development of GCC. First he must manage the process by which the funds are raised, and then drive the deal sourcing, transaction management and subsequent process by which value will be added to the holdings. This is by no means a simple task. He certainly has his work cut out but he demonstrates a strong determination and willingness to find answers to difficult questions.

Simon Eaves is an individual from Standard Bank who has been involved in the launch of the fund from the start. Standard Bank is a specialist emerging markets bank that is developing a strong franchise with an international client base. It has also launched a number of other private equity funds worldwide.

CHAPTER FEATURETTE 2

– The key regional transaction: Aramex

Ultimately it is the individual deals that drive the development of the region. There is no better marketing strategy than doing deals. Sourcing them, working them, exiting them is the essence of what investors do. So what has been the seminal transaction to date in the Middle Eastern private equity landscape?

Perhaps the deal that remains first amongst equals in the Middle Eastern private equity market is the Abraaj Capital investment in Aramex, the regional logistics company. Those who worked on the deal might argue that it was exceptionally complicated but it was actually a classic example of a buy-out that was further developed through bolt-on acquisitions, before being groomed brilliantly for a well timed exit. Along the way it dramatically improved its profitability, added to the number of its employees and will one day become a *Harvard Business Review* or *McKinsey Quarterly* case study.

Founded in 1983, Aramex is the region's leading logistics and courier provider with a network of 132 offices in 34 countries. Aramex is the founding member and chair of the Global Distribution Alliance – which partners with other regionally focused logistics firms to allow for a greater global presence.

It was the first Arab company to list on the NASDAQ market in 1997. With its comprehensive multi-product offering, Aramex has become a one-stop total transportation solutions company for retail and wholesale customers worldwide.

Abraaj led a $65 million takeover – comprising $25 million in equity and $40 million in debt – for the business in January 2002. The business had sales of $117 million in 2001. With a strong and dedicated management team, a large client base and solid IT infrastructure in place, there was a high potential for fast organic growth and increased revenues. The rapid growth and fragmented nature of the transportation market provided attractive consolidation opportunities.

During the holding period, new incentive schemes were launched for management including an employee stock option plan and reduced overheads while simultaneously leveraging existing assets to service a greater number of clients. The manager assisted in identifying and structuring strategic acquisition in high-growth markets and acquired Memo Express, the largest domestic courier company in the UAE, and Jordan Distribution Agency. As a result, the company's performance during the holding period was enhanced significantly from January 2002-December 2004; EBITDA and net profits grew by 128 per cent and 196 per cent respectively. The company was exited via an IPO on the UAE Stock Exchange in 2005.

Fadi Ghandour, born in Beirut and raised in Jordan, is chairman and chief executive of Aramex and takes up the story: "I studied political science at George Washington University in DC. I came out of college and set up the business with my partner. We sat together and by accident were talking about things and different ideas. This one came up. There was very little knowledge of the industry in the region. FedEx had just got going in the region a couple of years before we began our business. Having come from the States, they were just starting to advertise heavily. The idea came. Why not do something similar in a region that is completely dry?"

Looking back on the first few years, Ghandour recognises that there was a degree of fortune at launching a business during a time of dramatic regional change. "It was a time of the Iran-Iraq war, the Civil War in Lebanon and total uncertainty in the region. That was a blessing in disguise. There was no foreign investment. This gave me a good chance to build the business slowly which is a godsend to an entrepreneur who does not have a lot of cash to work with."

The real turning point came after the liberation of Kuwait at the end of the first Gulf War in 1991. FedEx and UPS entered the region but by then the business had developed its own infrastructure and blue-chip client base. "The story of Aramex began post-1991. The region was regaining stability and we had developed business models that were working. We were maturing. This is when Dubai began to take off and we were right there to take advantage of the attention the region was receiving."

This presented new growth opportunities he decided in the mid-1990s to consider completing a private placement from high net worth individuals and institutions in the Middle East. The lack of appetite by local Middle Eastern institutions that were focused on net assets upset Ghandour. "There was not an appetite and there was no valuation appreciation. Our business model is not based on assets and that shows the people in the region were unable to value things other than tangible assets. People looked at us and asked: what buildings and land do you own? We only own clients and they are only with us so long as we service them well. This was very disappointing as the brand is strong in the region and it should get the attention inside the region rather than outside."

In a bid to source the funding to grow the business, it went for a NASDAQ listing. Ghandour says: "I did not know what a public listing would be. I did not know about disclosure, compliance, SEC stuff, and it is a tribute to the company that we could do it. We were raising $7 million on valuation of $30 million in January 1997. A year later, we did a secondary offering on NASDAQ raising $21m. We met our targets every quarter. We complied every quarter. We complied with all SEC requirements." In practice, what this meant was that a very strong cash-generative business was being exceptionally well-run and yet not receiving the valuation that people felt it deserved.

Ghandour says: "It was Arif Naqvi's idea. In the early summer of 2001 – before 9/11 – he approached me with the idea to acquire the company. My partner had been looking for an exit for his stake. Dumping the stock on the exchange would have killed the stock price. So a deal was constructed to buy the whole company, although everybody apart from William Kingson stayed in the business."

A deal was organised valuing the business at $62 million of which $25 million was in equity and $37 million was through the issue of leverage. Under the terms of the transaction Abraaj and its co-investors took a 68 per cent stake, Ghandour took 25 per cent and management took seven per cent.

It was the first time that Aramex had leverage. "The focus of the business shifted to cash flow. We needed to ensure we could meet our obligations to the banks," says Ghandour. The result was a decision to massively improve on its collection from 82 days to 63 days which improved a hefty amount of cash and cleaned up a lot of debts. Secondly, a new bonus scheme was set up for country managers based on profitability, cash-flow and margin enhancements.

Fadi Ghandour says: "We had incredible discipline before we did the deal. We had rigorous systems with monthly reports. This was a well-run company and so it was not overly onerous to do what Abraaj wanted. This meant reporting monthly accounts four days earlier, but we continued to run the business as if we were still on NASDAQ. We issued press releases each quarter explaining how we were doing and demonstrated our professionalism."

The core business was robust. Consequently it quickly was in a position to make further acquisitions. The first was MemoExpress, the largest competitor to Aramex in the UAE, and the second was the Jordan Distribution Agency, which is the largest and most dominant magazine and newspaper distributor in the region. This transformed the business by opening up a new market for it.

"Memo was a turnaround deal," says Ghandour. "It added about five to six per cent to our bottom line. Jordan distribution agency was also a turnaround job – maybe two per cent added to our bottom line. We added eight to nine per cent to our bottom line through those two deals." After the two deals businesses had been integrated, in 2004, exit discussions began. "In summer 2004 we began talking about the possibility of doing an IPO on the Dubai financial markets. It went public earlier this year in July 2005. The company that went public was called Arab International Logistics, which then acquired Aramex for $190 million."

So what are the key lessons that Ghandour and his management team learnt from completing this seminal buyout transaction? "I learnt about leverage which had a huge impact. I also understood the approach to management that private equity firms bring. I also valued the knowledge of doing deals that Abraaj brought. We may be good operators but we are not financial operators. We learnt how to negotiate with banks, restructured loans. We learnt the discipline of managing the company with debt. We appreciate the value of debt."

The ultimate impact on the financial performance of the business was great. In the year to December 2005, sales were $235 million, compared with $189 million in 2004. Profits practically doubled – to $19 million.

Arif Naqvi of Abraaj says: "This deal showed private equity work at its best. We saw that it was listed on NASDAQ and believed there was no reason for it to be listed. It had superb cash-flows and was trading on a multiple of nine. The plan was built around repaying the debt within four years and we delivered."

Naqvi says: "We did this by closely aligning the management team with ourselves. When it listed on the UAE Stock Exchange we got six times our money back. The company is today quoted at $1 billion and so there was a clearly defined way of adding value. During the investment due diligence process we develop a 100-day plan. Without this you do not have the springboard to follow through once the deal is completed."

There are wider lessons to be learnt from this process. "Private equity is very important for developing entrepreneurship," says Ghandour. "Venture capital is what drives entrepreneurship. I am very worried that there is not enough money willing to take risks in the region. In my next life, I will become a venture capitalist. The region needs it. You do not need a lot of money. There are a lot of businesses that need support."

Chapter 5

How private equity will contribute to the future of the region

FORWARD FEATURES

What will the state of the Middle Eastern capital markets look like in 2020? Where will its regional economy get to and what role will its private equity protagonists be playing?

Will it go through the classic cycle of other emerging markets? Can it short-circuit the process? Will it fulfil the hopes of Prince Fahad in Saudi Arabia, Rachid Mohammad Al Rachid in Egypt and countless others across the region in finding a sustainable solution to its employment issues?

Economic liberalism may herald a new spring in the region, but seasons have a habit of evolving. Spring today can quickly become winter tomorrow. History is littered with the hopes of emerging countries dashed on the rocks of ambition and an inability to execute grand ambitions. So the onus is on leaders across all parts of the economic spectrum to generate results that deliver, are sustainable and do more than make the already wealthy business elite richer still.

However, the second half of 2006 should mark a period of optimism in the region. A report by the Economist Intelligence Unit argues that the MENA region will become one of the fastest growing in the world during the next two years. It expects the region to generate an average GDP growth of five per cent.

David Butter, author of the report and senior economist for the EIU in the region, says: "The fundamental driver of the region's growth will be the central importance of the Middle East to the global energy market. The Gulf States have also made significant strides in diversifying their economies so that a larger portion of oil and gas surplus revenue is invested within the region."

There are emerging shoots of companies using their regional strength as a launch pad to international expansion. SABIC recently launched a European arm and Dubai Ports World won control of P&O, the FTSE 100 stalwart, albeit without its US operations, following a nasty bout of protectionism and racism from the United States.

Regional observers are quick to point out the strength of Saudi Arabia, dynamism of the UAE, gas resources of Qatar and diversified economy in Egypt as evidence of progress.

Long-term crystal-ball gazing is more difficult and is rarely a profitable occupation; but this book feels it must attempt to make some concluding remarks given the research undertaken and the interviews conducted.

What follows will no doubt give rise to scorn being heaped upon the author in times to come. But the first four chapters have been a snapshot of a moment in time and so these final pages are intended to provide some future thoughts.

- The GCC ruling families will pursue further economic liberalisation without seeking to seed political control. They will slowly evolve to become regulators of business rather than owners. This will lead to a competitive push by Middle Eastern governments to constantly review their regulatory frameworks and as a by-product, an active market for international regulators who wish to work in these regions.

- Ruling families will examine new structures for their investments and holdings. Will Dubai Holding become the new model by which these families consider holding their assets along the lines of a traditional conglomerate structure? Maybe some of these ruling families will follow the trend set by Dubai Holding and consolidate their interests in more structured ways even if some errant members of families continue to view assets owned by their state as their personal jewels. More fundamentally the shift towards absorbing best practice corporate governance thinking on what they do will grow.

- The region must nurture a larger middle class and use changes in the education system to fuel this development in tandem with economic reforms. There will be a greater distribution of wealth and a continuing review of the education systems employed across the region, for education is a nation's future. The ruling families will recognise that a strong middle class will enable a more stable environment, as opposed to one that continues to rely heavily on patronage. It will however only be possible to deliver this through undertaking a determined push, which is likely to involve social reforms as much as political and economic ones.

- The region's merchant families will be actively encouraged to review the structures of their businesses, hire best of breed international managers who are incentivised in more Western styles of remuneration and list assets on the local stock markets. These families will make use of international consultants and banks to provide advice and slowly begin the long walk towards a more contemporary structure. Globalisation is changing the outlook of these businesses in seminal fashion and there will be a war for talent for best of breed international managers.

- This war for talent will become more complicated as other emerging markets – not least Asian ones such as India and China – are able to persuade mobile leaders to make new roots in their markets. Secondly, the Middle East's regional reliance on Indian brain-power will come under pressure as a vibrant domestic Indian market will provide a natural home for people who had previously migrated to the Gulf for economic opportunities.

- The region's demographic growth, coupled with the ability to invest surplus capital in non-oil related revenues, will trigger a sustained consumer boom. This will provide a number of opportunities for international multinationals. They will look to re-examine the terms of their franchise and licence agreements with the leading trading families and make decisions on whether they should bring the Middle East in-house. This will happen over the next two decades, giving the major trading families a short window to re-examine their portfolios and focus on the businesses which are wholly-owned subsidiaries and are not contracts with third-party brands.

- Saudi Arabia will evolve slowly but eventually overtake the UAE as the regional hub for business. Consequently it will introduce a number of reforms related to the entry and exit requirements for international business people. What remains a generally unpleasant experience for people merely seeking to do their job will become easier. However, the Gulf will remain resolutely focused on increasing the numbers of Saudis in the workforce. This will lead to ever more women joining the ranks of those employed, which will in generations to come lead to an improved work ethic amongst Saudi males. A by-product of all of this will be the visible sight of women driving cars in Saudi Arabia within three years.

- Women will enjoy an improved status and role throughout the region. The political nature of gender relations is likely to change and be driven by other more economic and commercial demands. The manner in which women participate in the public sphere will develop at different speeds in different countries but it is going one way – inexorably forward – as it should and needs to if the opportunities and fresh thinking are to be grasped. Ultimately it will be a simple case of mathematics. The equation goes like this: the release of potential for half the population in the Arab world will contribute to a better society. Therefore the reform agenda will begin to incorporate this within its agenda.

- The real estate developments in Dubai will continue to become ever more outlandish. For the next two decades many businesses will prefer to base themselves in the UAE and work across the region, but this will gradually slow and people will shift towards basing themselves in Saudi Arabia. The property boom will correct itself whilst their will be a steadier boom in the price of commercial real estate in Jeddah and Riyadh.

- The Arab-speaking region is likely to become the best performing emerging markets hub for equities in the world for the next five years. Companies will be boosted by the development of a single currency, slated to be launched in 2010, and easier trading relationships. The sheer amount of capital ready to be invested in new floats will soak up the stock for hundreds of new companies. Many of these will be family-backed as families develop a taste for selling to the capital markets, given their inability to be seen to sell to each other.

- The calibre of people in the region will increase and these will be globally astute individuals who are comfortable working in any part of the Eastern and Western world. The region's companies will invest more of their money in the education and training of their staff to global standards.

PRIVATE EQUITY SPECIFIC FORECASTS:

- The Asian and Middle Eastern continents will become the second most important centre of private equity investing, on a global basis, by 2020. The influence of Asia on determining developments in global trends in private equity will be huge. What has historically been a wind that blows from the East and West coasts of America will go in multiple directions, including Asia and Europe.

- Private equity firms will become even more specialised in their bid to demonstrate distinguishing features. For instance, with so many people under 30 in the Middle East, it will only be a matter of time before a new fund is launched that is focused on investing in the education sector.

- The CMA in Saudi Arabia and its counterparts across the region will produce rulings that support the structure of venture capital and buyout funds in the style that is operated in the West. These are based on partnership agreements between the limited partner and the general partner that manages the fund. This must happen if there is any aspiration to attract an international investor base into regional funds.

- Saudi Arabia will emerge as a key private equity market in its own right. It is the only nation in the region with a domestic market that is large enough to provide a sizeable market for business development. A growing number of funds that are currently based in Dubai will open offices in Saudi Arabia whilst a number of new entrants will go straight to Saudi.

- Investor relations will become a more prominent feature of the DNA of private equity globally. The need to treat investors as partners, who are able to contribute to the due diligence process inherent in understanding what will or will not constitute a good deal, will become a key feature of IR in the modern world.

- Fast forward to 2020 and competition amongst the existing private equity investors will become much tougher. Whether Blackstone and Carlyle formally launch funds – and it certainly will boost the strength of their universal fundraising abilities – remains to be seen. What is true is that the likes of Morgan Stanley, Goldman Sachs and BNP Paribas are all expanding their investment banking arms in the region and all of these three have robust and powerful private equity arms attached.

- There will be three types of private equity investors in the Middle East. The first set will include a small number of premium international brands that have become private equity institutions in their own right. Just as there are now a small number of genuinely global investment banks – most speak with an American accent – that offer a range of services, so there will be a small number of firms that invest globally across markets and sectors. The likeliest constituents of this group include Carlyle Group and Blackstone from the United States, Permira and CVC from Europe and maybe a small number of others that have yet to fully form.

These firms will have an on-the-ground presence in the region and are likely to become some of the most sought after employers. These will be institutions in their own right that are not reliant on the activities of their dynamic founders. They will have developed succession plans within the context of long-term thinking about the future of their businesses. These funds will view the Middle East as a source of funding for their various investment activities and also as a source of deal flow. For instance, as energy and the environment become an ever more politicised debate, firms such as Carlyle will seek out opportunities that allow them to bridge their political, economic and commercial contacts in the region.

- The second set of investors will be regional specialists – currently manifested in the likes of Abraaj – who have a stated plan to bring global best practice to a niche region. Their focus is on having leading edge local and regional knowledge, exceptional relationships with the ruling, trading and expatriate families and the ability to position them as culturally attuned to the mores of the region.

  These investors have a window of opportunity over the coming five years, although they will face increased pressure from rivals with deeper pockets in times to come. International institutions are able to cherry-pick the brightest individuals for their teams and over time, as the auction process becomes more the norm for securing deals, these groups will come under pressure to pay higher prices irrespective of their own personal networks.

- The third type of investor will be sector focused funds. Currently the likes of Injazat and GCC are embarking on this approach in the region, but it is at a very nascent stage. There are international sector specialist funds already in the market. For instance there are a growing number of specialist sector investors in the West who bring their knowledge and connections within a sector to bear on their approach to deal-doing. Capital Z is a global investor that is focused solely on the financial services sector and Veronis Suhler is a global investor that is focused solely on the media sector.

  These organisations will over time start considering opportunities that emerge from the Middle East, alternatively presented as the Arabic-speaking world. Arabic is fast emerging as one of the top four languages in the world after English, Mandarin and Spanish. This will drive investors in certain sectors.

- These investors will be serviced by an ever higher calibre of advisers. The likes of Goldman Sachs, Morgan Stanley, Citigroup and other major international banks are expected to extend their operations in the region. The potential fees available from supplying privatisation services to governments, advising leading businesses who are operating in the region or who want to be, will run into the hundreds of millions over the coming decades. Meanwhile there is a whole slew of other consultancy services, such as auditing, tax advisory and management consulting that will grow dramatically.

Colin Taylor, managing director at **CSFB** who oversees its leveraged buyout business, says: "Credit Suisse has had a long history of interaction with Middle Eastern clients. But the bank's presence in that market is expanding. As the bank develops a greater presence in the Middle East we must look at the Middle East for investment. We are exploring some product ideas, which could include a dedicated Middle Eastern fund."

Abe Saad of Shuaa says: "Things are moving very quickly. Now you see every major institution in the region opening an office in Dubai. Names such as Goldman's and Morgan Stanley are in the process of opening and building out their teams in the region. Every bulge bracket firm needs to be here." The point is that in days gone by the best of breed advisers and bankers did not want to work in this region and would prefer New York or London. That will change and the quality of advice will grow dramatically over the coming years.

- A number of these banks are in the process of determining their long-term alternative assets strategies and many will blend them within their private banking operations. The nature of the Middle East means that a small number of individuals account for the majority of its wealth. Developing holistic wealth management products, including access to private equity products, will become a regular feature of their products. Private equity will become entrenched as a tool for high net worths to invest as well as one that businesses use to evolve.

Doubtless a number of these predictions will appear ridiculous in 14 years' time. But for the sake of argument, this final chapter is focused on examining what needs to happen for these generally positive developments to materialise.

Sometimes, events have a habit of getting in the way of the most thought through of strategies. For instance the bombing in Amman in November 2005 will have temporarily frightened some investors from considering entering the region. Six months on, it feels like it happened a long time ago, and the region's leaders are getting significantly better at how they confront terrorists and the negative impact they may make.

Emerging markets ultimately emerge. They overcome instability to forge ahead and this is what will happen in the Middle East. Ultimately a confluence of political, economic and social factors will precipitate the development of a thriving private equity market. But what happens if this is wrong; what happens if the region fails to grasp its opportunity? Then what an optimist views as spring breaking could turn into an uncomfortable winter of discontent.

IF SPRING TURNS TO WINTER

The region remains long on financial capital, but is hopelessly short on human capital. It will take exceptional levels of hard work and brain-power to maximise the opportunity. Arguably the region resembles a home that is built on wafer-thin foundations.

His Excellency Dr Bassem Awadallah says: "The events in Iran, Palestine and Iraq give much thought to the politicians. So too does the fact that only 60 per cent of the Arab world is literate."

Beneath the upper echelons of educated society is a deep well of ignorance that lacks the wherewithal to grasp its opportunity.

There are a large number of reasons for this. First, there are relatively low levels of tertiary education in the local populations and a lack of exposure to a best practice business culture. The bulk of economic activity in the region is also dominated by public sector enterprises, which usually hire local nationals in order to combat rising unemployment levels.

Family groups dominate the private sector and talented professionals have restricted career growth prospects as the senior executive positions are frequently reserved for family members. In addition, because these groups have often increased revenues and profits on the back of strong government support, they have often functioned with low-calibre staff. Their approach has been to reward loyalty rather than performance and invest very little in developing their human capital.

Moreover, strict sponsorship rules allowing employers to restrict mobility within the workforce, has discouraged highly-skilled and ambitious labour from working in the region for significant periods.

The generally poor "brand" associated with the region has meant that it has been viewed as a relatively undesirable destination for talented knowledge workers. Frequently, the region has acted as a stepping-stone for such workers as they migrate towards the European and North American markets, or else as a short-term posting by workers from developed markets that see a stint in the region as being strictly a two to three-year affair. Salaries are no longer competitive with comparable positions in the West and the marketplaces are very different. As Iyad Duwaji, CEO of Shuaa Capital, points out: "You cannot bring a successful person from London to Dubai and expect them to be an instant success in a new business climate."

And, of course, the usual problems with relocation – schooling, spousal objections, cultural dislocation, loss of contact with family and friends – are all prevalent. Whilst the luxury of Dubai is a lure for some, there are still limits to the extent to which a warm climate, immaculately tailored golf courses and glamorous bars can atone for these losses.

Nonetheless, solutions to some of these obstacles do exist. Some countries have started to recognise the dearth of local talent and have taken initiatives to improve the situation. In Qatar, Cornell University and a private foundation formed by the Emir of Qatar are setting up a Medical

College. Governments in the GCC are also seeking ways to create employment for the locals within the private sector by imposing quotas on private sector companies hiring nationals.

Moving forward, this will be seen as a crucial theme. Private equity firms give a very high weighting to the availability of a high-quality talent pool. Because of their need to create value early on, they cannot tolerate inefficiency and sub-standard skill sets. Access to a well-qualified and competitive human resource pool is therefore of paramount importance.

There are also problems concerning investment opportunities in the region. Whilst recent years have witnessed a significant return of capital to the region, local economies have struggled to absorb significant amounts of this extra liquidity. As such, the challenges the region faces are more to do with a dearth of effective "users of capital" than of "capital providers", and, as discussed in Chapter 3, a poor nexus between the providers and the users. If these issues can be overcome, there is a more than adequate supply of capital in the region.

However, the most significant obstacle to private equity development remains cultural. Cultural barriers often stand in the way of divestments or partnerships with outsiders from family groups and regional governments. In addition, control and reputation issues still play a significant role in making business decisions. At a wider cultural level, private equity professionals complain of the same problems that Westerners generally encounter in an Arab business culture. Many talk about the cultural implications of the festivals of Eid and Ramadan, or the lethargic effects of a long, hot summer. Other are more specific in their criticisms, citing an *"in sha' allah"* (God willing) mentality in which important details are left to chance, or put off until an unspecified future date. Turnaround times are noticeably slower than in the West; it can take up to six months to negotiate a deal.

There are a number of other minor obstacles which should also be borne in mind. A possible reversal of liberalisation policies is not out of the question. Regional governments could take a short-term view and seek to delay the changes required in the regional economies by relying on their oil revenues to delay reform and economic liberalisation. There is also the danger of over-regulation or investment restrictions imposed by governments in the region, perhaps forcing funds to utilise sub-optimum structures in domiciles with poor legal or regulatory protection, or imposing unreasonable restrictions on capital or the ability of companies to source high-class human capital for key positions.

Political restrictions still exist, too. There is continuous lobbying by significant vested interests in the region to prevent change and to contain economic power in the hands of a few well-connected individuals or families. However, as Brad Bourland at **SAMBA** says: "There is a general tradition in Saudi Arabia that what you do with your money is your own business."

More significant is the possibility of increased competition and diversification within the industry in the future. On the one hand, the failure of high-profile private equity transactions in the region would have an impact on the credibility of the industry at this early stage in its development. In the short term, success stories are a critical feature in building the reputation of the industry in the region. The flip side of this is that, if there are a number of high-profile private equity success stories in the region, there is a very real threat of a multitude of copycat players entering the market with little or no real ability to perform. This may significantly impact both acquisition prices and, in the medium term, the credibility of the industry as a whole.

Success stories would go a long way to helping educate the key family businesses about the merits of working with private equity firms. One private equity investor says: "My uphill battle on a daily basis is trying to promote private equity while facing obstacles: the perceptions, apprehensions, myths, the risks, the perceived greed and incompetence of family controlled companies. Many of these companies think: who are you to tell me how to run my company?"

He adds that a lot of the trading families are apprehensive as they do not appreciate all the different ways to bring in talent. This may mean bringing in new management that can manage better than say a cousin, who is the general manager. "Once we convince one family and we have a success story then we move a step forward. Word gets around; one guy tells his cousin or a friend, and then he tells another. But if we make a mistake then we move two steps back. It's going to take a long time. Deal flow is still sporadic and we can't even say that there's an industry here."

The fear of opportunity risk is playing a negative part in the evolution of some family companies. Showing a path to how a family can improve an asset and then, for argument's sake float the business on a large valuation, often brings the same response. "Many senior members of the family say 'What should we do with $500m in cash when we have an asset that works?' Investing it would generate its own set of headaches." Consequently there are those who believe the Middle East resembles – in some instances – the United States of a century ago where families with the wealth and vision of the likes of the Rockefellers and Carnegies are investing in infrastructure, which will help the economy grow.

However globalisation means that today's Middle East just does not have the same amount of time that 19th Century America did. Eventually its oil wells will run dry and it will go on the quickest journey back in time imaginable. *Syriana,* the Oscar-winning film that attempts to portray the confluence of oil, military and political interests has a key scene in which a protagonist predicts that when oil runs out, the Middle East people will return to a 19th Century lifestyle. Somehow I doubt this. But more importantly a population, which is currently supine, will become angry and dispossessed – and so the time for action is now.

The region has no choice but to embrace every opportunity to move forward and so it must focus on the core priorities which includes giving greater encouragement to the very people who can develop a diversified future that is not dependent on oil.

THE IMPORTANCE OF CORPORATE GOVERNANCE

Corporate governance has become a worldwide buzzword, synonymous with the operational management of company boards. Bob Monks, the US corporate governance guru and founder of the leading governance consultancy Institutional Shareholder Services, says: "Good corporate governance is linearly related to the generation of wealth. I believe that putting your money in an ungoverned company is like backing a doped horse."

At its heart, corporate governance can add huge value and provide a framework towards best practice. Corporate governance pertains to the way a board is structured, the way it behaves and the way it handles the company on behalf of whom it acts.

Ultimately governance blends self-regulation and discipline within the context of enshrined parameters defined by the national government. Consequently having appropriate regulations in place is key to the development of the region. The companies that operate must then be encouraged to do so to best practice.

Governance is not just applicable to quoted companies. It constitutes a vital part of the decision-making process for private equity firms too. Poorly governed companies do not make for good investment material. As Arif Naqvi of Abraaj Capital explains: "Corporate governance is the single most important confidence-enhancer for the investment community."

The focus on governance is a comparatively recent development, a consequence of increased sophistication on the part of investors and increasingly unrestrained behaviour on the part of company executives in the late 1990s. Institutional shareholders first began to look closely at the way companies were governed early on in that decade. The pace of development accelerated in the aftermath of the dotcom boom, as shareholders became more exercised about issues such as remuneration and director integrity.

Corporate collapses such as Enron and WorldCom in the US or Parmalat in Italy have encouraged shareholders around the world to be mindful of the way in which executives behave. The excessive licence awarded to directors in those companies is regarded as symptomatic of loose governance and is thought to have had a tangible link to their eventual demise. Western governments, regulators and shareholders have responded to these crises by attempting to tighten up the governance process.

In the US, the Securities and Exchange Commission has introduced the Sarbanes-Oxley Act, obliging companies to be far more rigorous in their financial and accounting disclosure. The Act sets down stipulations about the composition of listed company boards and obliges them to adopt far more stringent internal audit controls.

Improving board performance in emerging markets was the recent topic covered in a *McKinsey Quarterly* feature. It stated that in most emerging markets, the institutions that help guard against corporate malfeasance – securities regulators, stock exchanges, the judiciary, institutional investors, equity analysts, accountants and a probing media – are still relatively weak or lack critical mass. Boards may therefore be the most robust line of defence. Even more importantly, it noted that in a global investor opinion survey, equity investors will pay a premium of 20-40 per cent for emerging market companies with strong boards of directors.

Theory seems great but does it work in practice? Getting family-owned businesses to support board reform can be difficult. Many successful ones are still run by a founder who, having built the business from scratch, can be reluctant to dissolve authority to a professional board. As control of such companies passes to a younger generation that is usually more familiar with Western corporate governance practices, the level of support for effective and professional boards rises.

The study of corporate governance for private equity funds is a very new topic. During 2005 there was a debate that was ignited and is likely to develop over the coming years.

Jeremy Coller, founder of international private equity firm Coller Capital, launched it by giving a speech in London outlining an agenda for governance within private equity to an invited audience of industry leaders. This was one of the first occasions that someone from within the private equity industry had attempted to set some industry-wide standards to be followed.

He says: "Our industry now attracts a huge amount of public attention, but we cannot afford to be complacent. Sooner or later there will be a major scandal as a result of gross incompetence or downright dishonesty. When it happens this will probably lead to an over-reaction by heavy handed regulators."

He emphasised the repercussions in corporate regulation that stemmed from the scandals of Enron, WorldCom, and Robert Maxwell's pension fraud. He urged the industry to act now, "while times are good, before the horse has bolted. If we don't, corporate governance will get done". His comments are in marked contrast to those of industry pioneer Henry Kravis, co-founder of Kohlberg Kravis Roberts, who recently said the absence of any major scandal in a private equity- backed company was proof of the industry's enhanced standards of governance.

Private equity investors in the Middle East would do well to heed the words of Coller. Limited partners who have to make judgements about competing firms are likely to select those who take disclosure and transparency seriously. Ultimately greater openness builds trust with investors. Coller's mantra was focused on four key recommendations: "Private equity funds should be audited by a 'prestigious firm with deep pockets and a name to protect', which would become a natural check and balance."

Secondly, the use of custodians for private equity should be institutionalised, once again creating a natural check and balance as no custodian would want to tarnish their name by activities that bring the industry into disrepute.

Coller also recommended the introduction of "no fault divorce clauses" which would mean that investors could dissolve a partnership. He said in the past it had been impossible to "kill" managers.

Finally, he advocated the abolition of deal-by-deal carry, where managers share in the profit throughout the life of the fund, rather than at the end of the fund. He said it was incredibly difficult to get money back "from people who had already spent it and paid tax on it".

The debate is only just beginning but investors in the Middle East must decide on what benchmarks they want to develop their own industry by. Nonetheless, corporate governance is becoming an issue in the Gulf region. As financial and commercial structures evolve, there is a growing belief that it is time to be more rigorous in the creation and application of principles or rules to which companies should adhere.

"Business in the Middle East tends to revolve around relationships and trust but there is an understanding that governance is becoming more important," says Anne Simpson, executive director of the International Corporate Governance Network.

What is driving this nascent development? Markets are opening up to competition, governments are becoming more liberal in their approach to business and many states have started to privatise their assets. "This has all given impetus to the corporate governance process," says Simpson.

Another perspective is to recognise the increased power of the institutional investor. At a time when numerous emerging markets are keen to take public assets private – selling off shares to the international investors – there is a need and recognition to play by their games. So if you want Fidelity or Merrill Lynch to buy and hold your shares, you are going to recognise the requirement to listen to your potential investors.

Their shopping list of requirements is extensive. But as Simpson says: "There has been an enthusiastic response to the idea of greater internal controls and more rigorous accounting and auditing procedures."

Exemplifying this trend, the Global Corporate Governance Forum, a joint venture between the World Bank and the Organisation for Economic Co-operation and Development, organised two events within a few months of each other in early 2005, both on corporate governance issues in the Middle East.

The Centre for International Private Enterprise, a non-profit affiliate of the US Chambers of Commerce, has also devoted time and resources to the Gulf and the Levant, compiling a special report on corporate governance in the Middle East in the spring of 2005.

The topic emerged again in a report produced by the Portland Trust – the think tank set up in 2004 by Sir Ronald Cohen who founded global buyout firm Apax Partners – which commissioned Bladonmore to interview a number of entrepreneurs in the West Bank and Gaza in Palestine to ascertain their views on key issues.

The thinking and effort has not gone unnoticed by those who count. Lucy Ferguson, Equity Capital Markets director at Citigroup, says: "I have been pleasantly surprised by the levels of governance and internal management in the Gulf and the Levant. Many of the companies I have come across have better practices than other emerging market corporates."

Underlining the commitment of the region to the governance arena, in May 2005, the Islamic Financial Services Board arranged a two-day summit in Doha, looking at governance and accountability under the banner "The Rise and Effectiveness of Corporate Governance in the Islamic Financial Services Industry". The Summit offered regulators, supervisors and market players the opportunity to deliberate on topical corporate governance issues.

The IFSB itself was only formed three years ago, specifically to address governance concerns. The organisation describes itself as "an international standard-setting body of regulatory and supervisory agencies that have vested interest in ensuring the soundness and stability of the Islamic financial services industry, which is defined broadly to include banking, capital market and insurance.

In advancing this mission, the IFSB will promote the development of a prudent and transparent Islamic financial services industry by introducing new, or adapting existing, international standards consistent with Islamic Shari'ah principles, and recommend them for adoption. To this end the work of the IFSB complements that of the Basel Committee on Banking Supervision, International Organisation of Securities Commissions and the International Association of Insurance Supervisors." The formation of the IFSB and the work that it and other organisations are doing in the Middle East highlight the increased focus on corporate governance in the region.

In the private equity industry, as elsewhere in the commercial world, governance does not just revolve around disclosure and due diligence; it focuses too on the appointment of appropriate directors.

It is widely thought that five core factors contribute to good governance in this regard: the relationship between the board and the major shareholders; board composition; the qualifications of non-executive directors; the remuneration package for non-executive directors; and the existence of appropriate board committees.

A small board of between four to six directors tends to work best for private equity portfolio companies – the emphasis is on lean, mean business enterprises so there is no room for passengers. The board should, however, have at least two non-executive directors, one of whom is the chairman.

This focus on the board and its composition is of growing importance as competition in the sector becomes increasingly intense. Whereas private equity firms used to buy businesses, hold them and then sell them on a few years later, now they have to add value during the process. Frequently, therefore, they either change the management of portfolio companies or inject non-executive directors into these businesses or both. Many private equity firms now insist on having one or two of their own partners on the boards of portfolio companies or parachuting in experienced directors from elsewhere to oversee management procedure and strategy

Good non-executive candidates tend to share certain characteristics and qualifications. Seasoned practitioners have an understanding of the different circumstances and expectations of private equity investors. They tend to have a track record of successful achievement as managers in the private sector. They have been on boards before, but not necessarily as a non-executive director. They are ready and willing to assist the portfolio management team. They will often but not always have relevant industry experience. And they are financially literate.

Good people recognise the value of their time and charge for it. Normally, non-executive directors are invited to buy shares in the portfolio company either from the outset or after serving an appropriate probationary period, such as 12 months. Options to acquire shares and cash bonus payments on successful exit are extremely common forms of financial incentive. It is widely thought that the purchase of equity at a fair value early in the life of a portfolio investment is the simplest, most effective and most appropriate means of aligning the interests of the board and shareholders in both good times and bad.

Conor Kehoe, founder and director of McKinsey's private equity practice in Europe, recalls a conversation with a Scandinavian investor concerning the correct level of risk for directors to experience. "I want his yacht and his holiday home to be at risk," concluded the Scandinavian, "but not his main residence itself."

THE ROLE PLAYED BY NON-EXECUTIVE DIRECTORS

In this regard, there is a wide discrepancy between quoted and private equity enterprises. In the UK at least, companies are actively discouraged from offering share options or their ilk to non-executive directors. In private equity firms, the reverse is true.

The role of the non-executive director has become an increasingly significant focus of the corporate governance arena. Corporate collapses in the West have highlighted the role that a non-executive can play. If they are absent or negligent, the executive members of the board can be allowed to run amok. If they are responsible and conscientious, they can prevent catastrophe.

In essence, a non-executive director should provide an effective foil to the executive element of a board. The non-executive director is expected to contribute to board meetings by providing an objective viewpoint.

Non-executive directors are encouraged for the most part to train their focus at board level and not concern themselves with the day-to-day affairs of management. This allows them to provide an independent and more high-level perspective. They are also expected to provide specialist experience and contribute towards strategic development. The best in breed have a broad knowledge of the industry with which their company is associated. They can, in addition, facilitate relationships with third parties and raise the company's profile.

Non-executive directors are expected to take responsibility for monitoring the performance of executive management. If executives falter or fail, it is the job of the non-executives to alert the rest of the board to the situation and deal with it promptly and appropriately. As Mark Mobius, emerging markets fund manager at the investment institution Templeton Asset Management, points out: "Sitting on a board can be very time-consuming."

The *McKinsey Quarterly* report on the subject highlighted one financial institution that convened a board meeting 19 times in 2004, each lasting five to seven hours, because very few matters had been delegated to management. It says: "Areas that would normally be its preserve are often handled by boards in emerging markets because experienced executives are in short supply or boards don't fully trust the executives they actually have."

Both non-executives and executive directors are expected to ensure that the company accounts presented to its shareholders are a true and fair reflection of its actions and financial performance, and that the necessary internal control systems are implemented and monitored regularly. A non-executive director has an important part to play in fulfilling this responsibility.

Another of the board's crucial functions is to decide on new appointments to the board and other senior positions in the company. In some cases, this is done within a dedicated nominations committee, composed of executive and non-executive directors, whose task it is to ensure that appointments are made according to agreed specifications. Even if there is not a dedicated committee, however, non-executives are considered a vital part of the recruitment process, ensuring that the best directors are appointed, rather than those who simply happen to be friends of the chief executive.

THE MIDDLE EASTERN APPROACH

In the Gulf and Levant region, the role of the non-executive is at an embryonic stage. Some businesses, such as Abraaj Capital, have a full complement of non-executives and understand the expertise that these board members can bring. Others tend to be less clear about the point of non-executives. And in some instances, even if non-executives have been appointed, they do not do the job required. One regional chief executive complained: "They meddle when they're not wanted and then go away on holiday when they're actually needed."

There may not be universal agreement across the Middle East on the role and importance of non-executive directors or the depth and importance of governance – one imagines a number of senior business leaders in the Gulf viewing non-executives as akin to decorations – but the next generation of business leaders are acutely aware and appreciative of the value they bring. This is one debate that has huge significance in the region.

Anne Simpson of the International Corporate Governance Network believes that the governance debate in the Gulf and the Levant has a relevance that stretches far beyond its remit in the West.

"Financial liberation is being seen in some quarters as a first step towards political liberation. If corporate and financial structures are becoming more transparent and open, there is a hope that political structures will follow suit," she says. Simpson also suggests that private equity firms are leading the way in this particular regard.

"For private equity firms, management oversight and investor protection are a given. Even if they do not see themselves as champions of corporate governance, they pursue its underlying philosophies almost instinctively," she says.

Looking to the future, private equity could well prove a catalyst for improved corporate governance in the region: as a rule of thumb, private equity firms will only invest in companies with sound, transparent accounting practices. If local firms want to woo private equity investment, they will have to ensure their accounts are up-to-date and comprehensive. Increasingly, they will have to focus more on performance than patronage.

THE IMPACT OF ECONOMIC CHANGE ON ISLAMIC BANKING AND ROLE OF INTERNATIONAL M&A

Private equity will contribute to the wave of change that impacts boards in the region over the coming times. However, it will also be part of the process that triggers evolving developments in Islamic banking. Arif Usmani, chief risk officer of SAMBA Financial Group, says: "I am sure the new entrants (Goldman Sachs, Morgan Stanley etc.) will all come with new products that we will consider distributing to our customers."

This is not to suggest that the incumbent operators do not have the innovation to develop their own products, but it underlines the blending of tradition and modernity as Islamic finance gets a 21st century makeover.

For instance, when Dubai Ports World made its offer to acquire P&O in the UK, the intention was to launch a $2.8billion chunk of funding from Islamically structured instruments, making it the largest ever. This was being arranged by Dubai Islamic Bank and Barclays Capital. The regional banks in the Gulf lack the depth to arrange such amounts, making it sensible for them to partner with international groups on a deal-by-deal basis.

Islamic finance looks poised to grow globally and follow its customers as they embark on more international merger and acquisition style transactions. This is likely to provide further opportunities for private equity firms that have regional investments as they will be able to encourage them to widen their horizons.

The burden does not fall exclusively on the shoulders of the leading families. Banks and suppliers of Islamic finance products also need to raise their standards to match the times. In the West it is the debt markets that fuel private equity. In the past, one of the perceived obstacles to economic modernisation in the Arab world was the rule governing the receipt of interest. In recent decades, however, this difference between Arab and Western practice has been overcome by the development of Islamic banking.

Islamic finance is constrained by a unique set of guidelines which is established by scholars according to the principles of Shari'ah – an organic law common to all Muslims. Shari'ah imposes an explicit moral framework which channels capital away from investments considered "haram" (sinful).

Shari'ah law itself is derived from a range of overlapping sources: the Koran; the Sunna / Hadiths (the sayings and experiences of the Prophet Muhammad); Qiyas (analytical comparison); Ijtehad (reasoning and logic applied by scholars); and Ijmaa (a consensus on issues requiring Ijtehad).

According to Shari'ah, investments in companies that manufacture haram goods such as alcohol, tobacco or pork products are forbidden. As such, the entertainment industry as a whole – hotels, casinos, cinemas, music – is off-limits. Shari'ah investment principals also exclude companies linked to weapon manufacturing, human cloning, abusive animal testing and abortion.

Through private equity, particularly through early-stage investing, institutions may participate in, and benefit from, the growth of companies as partners rather than as creditors.

However, venture capital investments allow for even greater clarity in decision-making as well as more control over the agenda laid out by the portfolio company. From a Shari'ah point of view this is the "purest" form of investment. A board can be appointed to establish screens on what investments are acceptable and the type of securities that can be used to finance companies. For example, convertible or preferred stock options are common in venture capital funds but are unacceptable in an Islamic context as they earn interest.

From a Shari'ah compliance standpoint, on the other hand, private equity is less "pure" in nature as it tends to be invested in more mature businesses. As these are in the later stages of development, bank loans are often a more common source of funding.

Naturally, there is some debate among Shari'ah scholars as to the application of Islamic financing. Buyout transactions and re-capitalisations obviously involve debt securities. Nonetheless, a properly structured leveraged buyout can be embraced by Islamic investors. Some investors view coupon-paying securities as permissible, as long as their structure cannot be viewed as a straight loan. A company that securitises its cash flow and sells the right to receive a portion of that flow, for example, would not be against the rules, according to some analysts.

These are, of course, grey areas. The line between a loan that pays interest and a security that channels cash flow is thin. A straight loan treats money as a commodity in its own right, rather than as a measure of value that has no human utility. A securitised cash flow, on the other hand, lays claim to the sale of underlying commodities or services. As such, the receiver of the cash flow is actually receiving his coupon based on the buying and selling of real commodities as opposed to a fee for the "rental" of an intrinsically valueless currency.

Loans are allowed under Shari'ah under three distinct circumstances: the lender does not intend to be repaid in full; the lender is simply "parking" money with the borrower for safekeeping and does not expect interest; or the lender is sending money in advance to the borrower with the expectation of sharing in profits or losses.

From a fixed income viewpoint, the third criterion bears the most resemblance to an unsecured, coupon-bearing note – the buyer may share in a pre-determined cash flow so long as the issuer performs at a certain level. Otherwise, both the note-holder and the issuer experience loss.

However, securitisation does create an imbalance between the issuer and the holder whereby fixed payments remain independent of the underlying performance of the assets. Shari'ah frowns on any form of imbalance in business relationships.

Despite these obstacles, it would seem that there are many opportunities for synergies between the private equity industry and Islamic financing. The website of the Al Rajhi Banking and Investment Corporation, the Saudi financial institution, has a comprehensive overview of the investment principles that guide Islamic banking.

It reads almost like an introductory guide to the private equity industry: "The basic and foremost characteristic of Islamic financing is that, instead of a fixed rate of interest, it is based on profit-and-loss sharing. Islam encourages Muslims to invest their money and to become partners in business instead of becoming creditors. This encourages entrepreneurship. In turn, entrepreneurs compete to become the agents for the suppliers of financial capital who, in turn, will closely scrutinise projects and management teams. The objective is that high-risk investments provide a stimulus to the economy and encourage entrepreneurs to maximise their efforts."

It is the development of regional equity markets, rather than the emergence of new Shari'ah compliant products, that is driving the excitement of many investors in private companies. Put simply, "Growth has been phenomenal," says Lucy Ferguson, Equity Capital Markets director at Citigroup.

Between 2000 and 2003, market capitalisations in the GCC grew at a Compound Annual Growth Rate (CAGR) of 48 per cent. In 1998, the UAE stock market was trading on a price to earnings ratio of more than 30. By last year, the price/earnings ratio had fallen to 16.8 and the dividend yield was just 3.11 per cent. Market commentators suggest this has all the hallmarks of a bubble.

There have been some spectacular examples, too, of the burgeoning popularity of local IPOs. In 2004, the UAE property finance company Amlak Finance launched an AED412.5 million public offering. The transaction was 33 times oversubscribed and the company received AED13.7 billion in commitments within ten days of the launch of its offering.

In early 2005, the UAE-based oil business Aba Petroleum floated on the stock market, aiming to raise $120 million. It ended up with subscriptions of $107 billion. Such oversubscription has never been witnessed in any country at any time before. "This is an unheard-of dynamic," says Ferguson.

Currently, flotations are handled entirely by local firms but the explosion in demand over the past year or two has encouraged international investment banks to flock to the region in search of opportunities. These developments have a significant impact on the way companies manage themselves. "As sources of finance become more sophisticated, people are waking up to the importance of transparency and openness," says business journalist Will McSheehey.

Most financial experts expect a flood of new IPOs to hit the region's stock markets over the coming months. Their optimism is boosted by such initiatives as the creation of the Dubai International Finance Centre (DIFC). Indeed, some international bankers regard the DIFC as the single most encouraging sign for the future development of capital markets in the Middle East.

THE BACKBONE OF POLITICAL STABILITY

At a very basic level private equity demands political stability to flourish. Stable and reasonably predictable macro-economic conditions are a prerequisite for successful private equity investment. In particular, stable currencies, low inflation, strong GDP growth and free capital flows are crucial. In this context the GCC countries score very highly. Most countries in the GCC have healthy foreign exchange reserves and positive economic outlooks.

The UAE, Kuwait and Qatar have excellent sovereign ratings and low external debt to exports ratios (less than 50 per cent for UAE, Saudi Arabia, Qatar and Kuwait), signalling overall economic stability. Furthermore, strengthening oil prices provide an additional boost to their revenue base in the short term. These factors alone should present a significant level of reassurance to US dollar denominated investors.

The ability to create liquidity within a three-to-seven-year time frame is crucial to private equity groups – until investments are sold and cash returns generated for investors, the professionals running such funds are paid relatively little. Their upside is tied to the investors' upside. The growing acceptability of merger and acquisition activity in the region (perhaps most advanced in Kuwait), coupled with an increased emphasis on the development of the regional stock markets, indicate that exit routes in the region are beginning to develop. However, progress still needs to be made. In this regard private equity funds can help to create listable companies and thereby play an important role in the development of the region's stock markets.

Compliance with the World Trade Organisation is also a significant factor in the ongoing economic development of the region. The GCC is a political and economic grouping which significantly eases the ability of its citizens to travel, own businesses and work in member countries. Yet despite signing an economic integration agreement in 1983, the GCC has not operated as a free-trade zone.

This year, however, intra-GCC tariff harmonisation is due to take place. In addition, over the past two to three years, the GCC has begun liberalising its laws in terms of entry, residency and ownership from non-GCC states. A symptom of this is that every target country has become a signatory to

WTO with the exception of Saudi Arabia, which is in the final stages of negotiation with the WTO. Kuwait and Bahrain signed up in 1995, UAE and Qatar in 1996 and Oman in 2000. A relatively small percentage of trade and commerce currently takes place between GCC countries (or other countries in the Middle East). Whilst this is largely due to the distorting effect of the significant energy exports to OECD countries and the concomitant import of goods produced in these countries, it does nonetheless highlight the relative paucity of inter-regional trade and industry.

It is thought that the ongoing move to WTO-compliant business regimes will increase regional integration. In particular, this may include projects in agency/distribution transformation, logistics, retailing and scale industries such as construction. WTO compliance will also gradually create a more attractive environment for foreign companies through tariff reduction, change of ownership laws, fairer competition and better dispute settlement.

This is a positive overview. A less positive perspective comes from examining the whole of the Middle East in its entirety.

Ultimately private equity is a business that is focused on assessing risk. Deal-doers make daily judgments about the risks facing an industry, company or management team, but do not like having to judge a country. The recent bombs in Jordan will deter both limited partners who might invest in private equity funds and those individuals, such as the Masri brothers, who operate private equity management companies. The question marks hanging over the Syrian governments involvement in Lebanon is another black mark on a region that could do with a few decades of peace and stability to promote economic prosperity.

So long as political unrest continues the region will not realise its potential. It would be naïve and inappropriate to suggest that political instability will reduce substantially during the next 15 years.

Optimists will hope that rapprochement – driven by a greater level of understanding towards the Middle East – will develop between the G8 political elite and the Middle East governments, which share a symbiotic relationship. Developments in the creation of a viable Palestinian state that can co-exist with Israel will also contribute to stability and therefore economic growth. Second guessing that area is not the task of this book, however. If economic ambitions are to be realised, there is a need for the wider Middle East to learn some lessons about the opening up of markets and minds from their cousins in the Gulf.

For instance, within the UAE there is an appetite to turn the UAE into a global hub for a number of industries. His Highness Sheikh Mohammed Bin Rashid Al Maktoum wants to place Dubai in the same breath as London, New York and Shanghai. Realistically it has more likelihood of becoming a 21st century Singapore. Ultimately the UAE will be the regional hub for private equity in the Middle East. It already is, helped in no small part by the sympathy from the ruling families in the UAE to support this development, as evidenced by the creation of Dubai International Capital, which is one of the most high-profile new private equity firms to launch in the past year.

However, the pace of development throughout the wider Gulf and Middle East is distinctly slower. Saudi Arabia, the engine of so much of the region's growth, might be accelerating ahead in terms of its equity markets, but it is proving to be slothful in terms of the development of new private equity funds.

So it is more realistic to suggest the region will develop incrementally rather than through a series of giant leaps forward.

Nonetheless private equity will act as a fountain of opportunity for economic growth. Given the opportunity – and it does exist – it will assist governments, banks, investors, business managers and family groups to maximise the value of their assets, and then deliver a sustained improvement in the operating performance of the businesses which it owns.

Ultimately the economic benefits of private equity will overcome historic reticence to embrace the asset class. Governments will benefit from economic diversification, the growth in employment opportunities generated by private equity firms, improved terms of trade and value creation. Regional banks could benefit from the development of their corporate lending businesses and the emergence of the acquisition finance departments, which is estimated to be worth billions of dollars over the next five years.

So what should governments do to promote private equity in the short term?

First they must create and enforce legal and regulatory frameworks that foster an investment friendly climate. Once again the UAE is leading the way in this regard. It has made a concerted effort to set up the legal and regulatory institutions required. For instance, the Dubai International Finance Centre (DIFC) was conceived by the government of Dubai in February 2002 and the federal cabinet of the UAE decreed the following year that the DIFC should be established as a financial free zone. The market was finally and formally opened in 2005.

The DIFC's remit was to create a regional capital market with world-class regulations and standards. The Centre is also expected to generate 50,000 jobs by 2007 and it aims to offer participants an attractive investment environment, including 100 per cent foreign ownership, zero tax on income and profits and the freedom to repatriate capital and profits without restrictions. The DIFC is governed and regulated by international laws, the working language of the DIFC is English and the trading currency is US dollars.

Leading executives in the region suggest that the aim is to create. "London in the Desert" and the DIFC itself describes its guiding principles as "integrity, transparency and efficiency".

Comprising 45 buildings on a 110-acre site in the main centre of Dubai valued at $1 billion, the DIFC contains office, residential, retail and hotel accommodation. His Highness Sheikh Mohammed serves as president of the DIFC. Initially, there are six core sectors of activity: banking services; capital markets; asset management and fund registration; reinsurance; Islamic finance; and back-office operations.

International reaction has been extremely positive. The International Herald Tribune described the DIFC as a "shot in the arm for regional markets".

Graeme Muir, international managing partner at Norton Rose in Dubai, said the DIFC should represent an attractive option to regional family groups, allowing them to keep control of their business whilst simultaneously raising capital on the open exchange.

The centre has been well received by a number of financial institutions too. Thirty leading international firms, including Deutsche Bank, Credit Suisse and Standard Chartered, have applied for licences. A significant development recently was the licencing of Abraaj Capital by the Dubai Financial Services Authority (DFSA), the regulatory body of the DIFC. This was important because Abraaj is a regional firm, and came from an environment that was unregulated by any central bank, making it the first such organization to be licenced by the DIFC, a move which augers well for the regional private equity industry as more and more firms will offer themselves up for regulatory scrutiny.

David Knights of HSBC Private Equity says: "It will be very good for the long term. The most important thing will be the introduction of the exchange, which should encourage more businesses to operate and list there and stimulate more exit activity."

Letters of intent have been received from Aon, an insurance brokering and risk management consulting organisation, and Permal Group, one of the leading multi-manager hedge fund groups. Al Salam Group, a Saudi Arabian development company, has invested $150 million in purchasing the building that will house the DIFC. The Dow Jones has reached an agreement with the DIFC to launch a Dow Jones DIFC Arabia Titans 50 index of the region's blue-chip companies. A memorandum of understanding has also been signed with a number of international firms to ensure clearing and settlement is conducted with maximum efficiency.

Once fully operational, the DIFC will constitute three core divisions: the DIFC Development Authority, the DIFC Land Company and the Dubai International Financial Exchange (DIFX). The Development Authority is the holding company for the DIFC and the Land Company is the financial district, where DIFC licensees will operate. It is currently under construction and will be completed by the end of the decade.

The DIFX has been specifically created to provide a larger and more liquid securities market than currently exists in any of the region's national exchanges. The fully electronic marketplace will trade a range of securities including equities; index funds and unit investment trusts; futures, options and other complex derivatives; commodities, such as oil and gold; and alternative risk products. Significantly, too, Islamic-compliant structured products will be traded, as will bonds and other debt-related instruments.

Governments must also accelerate the pace of privatisations. Businesses that are ultimately run for the benefit of shareholders achieve better results than those run on behalf of government ministries. They are more efficiently run, invest profits, create employment opportunities and pay taxes which contribute to the national development. Ultimately governments must confront a philosophical question: do they exist to be the major employer and supplier of services or do they exist to govern?

A number of Middle Eastern governments are watching the actions of the Egyptian government closely. It has decided to tentatively begin a privatisation process for a number of its assets beginning with Telecom Egypt, the largest business in the country. The process is not without its issues: taking a business that has been state-run for generations and gearing it up to be ready to confront the international markets forces the company to question its strategy and planning. But ultimately better businesses emerge.

Akil Hamed Beshir, chairman of Telecom Egypt, says: "Egypt is a promising country. It has attractive GDP growth, a stable political and economic environment and Telecom Egypt is the jewel in the crown of its companies." Interestingly state privatisations have become a barometer for the commercial well-being of a country. The international financial community is doing its best to ensure the companies are prepared accordingly.

"Telecom Egypt will be able to satisfy all types of investors. For those seeking a regular dividend the business has the necessary cash flow to satisfy investors and it is also growing rapidly for those who want exposure to a growth stock," says Hamed Beshir, demonstrating a degree of determination to ensure the flotation is a success.

The pace of privatisation, public-private partnerships and public sector spin-outs of services should increase significantly. This process will achieve three critical objectives for governments: it will generate capital to shore-up government finances; it will pass through to the private sector the liability for reinvestment and development capital for these enterprises; and it will generate better and more efficient companies from which the economy as a whole will benefit.

It is currently estimated that the privatisation process in the GCC region has reached less than ten per cent of its potential. More than 600 companies have been recognised as potential targets representing a potential value of over $90 billion.

Private equity firms should be well positioned to benefit from an increase in the pace of privatisation programmes, since financial engineering, change management and clear strategic vision – which underpin private equity – are critical to the success of these transactions. Arif Naqvi of Abraaj says: "Private equity can be transformational capital. It can be the bridge from the public sector to a more commercial environment. We investors hold the ultimate power vis-à-vis regional governments."

The move to privatise is symptomatic of a region in search of answers. Over the next few years each of the GCC countries will face considerable challenges in terms of creating jobs, wealth and opportunities for their rapidly growing, youthful populations.

The challenge is particularly acute for Saudi Arabia, with the largest population in the region (22 million people) and conservative estimates of unemployment in excess of 15 per cent. Estimates suggest that in order to effectively manage the rising unemployment levels, approximately seven to nine million new jobs will have to be created across the Gulf and the Levant by 2020. This would represent an annual employment growth of 4 per cent – a feat unprecedented in economic history.

It is time for Middle Eastern governments to call in the experts. The most effective creators of employment are the private equity community. It has the ability to dramatically increase companies through organic and acquisitive growth. Each Middle Eastern government should invite a team of private equity specialists to contribute to its employment stimulation initiatives. The sense of urgency is becoming ever more apparent.

Government budgets across the region are now stretched and genuine employment in government entities is full to overflowing – the only solution is to create an environment in which the private sector can grow and provide wealth-creating employment opportunities on a scale that has seldom been achieved in the past.

It is now widely thought that private equity funds will be able to play a key role in addressing this problem. First, they will help to propel rapid growth within companies that will in turn lead to creation of new employment opportunities. Secondly, by focusing on improving operating efficiency, they will support the creation of a more talented workforce with diverse and enhanced skill sets. And thirdly, they will serve as a focal point for additional investment in companies and industries as they become genuinely competitive. The private equity industry already enjoys an impressive track record in stimulating employment opportunities.

THE ECONOMIC AGENDA

The domestic agendas of the Middle East nations are not immune from the forces of globalisation, which continues to dictate the economic agenda today. End users – wherever they are in the world – are demanding a better service at a cheaper price. It used to be enough for business managers to worry solely about their domestic markets but business has become borderless. Consequently the issues surrounding globalisation have an impact on all businesses.

Even the Middle East – renowned for having its own cultural way of doing business – recognises that it has to play according to global rules. Avi Bhojani, head of Bates Pan Gulf, part of the WPP network says: "The Middle East has a decision to make. Recognise the terms of reference that business demands on a global basis or stay within its own clique. It must choose the more demanding first route to growth."

Much of the responsibility for generating new employment opportunities currently resides on the shoulders of the trading families, who own the powerful conglomerates driving growth throughout the region. These families are spending time examining what the best structure is to propel their businesses into the 21st century. It might be as a publicly listed company on a regional stock exchange, merged with an industry rival

Family groups looking to divest non-core or distressed businesses can benefit through association with private equity firms since they can provide viable exits with minimum risk to the reputation of these families. More likely, given the lack of appetite by families to sell assets, will be the emergence of joint venture arrangements and co-investment initiatives between traditional trading families and private equity firms.

The private equity industry can provide business managers with opportunities to become partners in management buyouts or Greenfield ventures. Managers can offer industry knowledge, experience and expertise; private equity firms can provide funding capabilities and drive value creation. The managers who might previously have built careers based on earning an income from their endeavours will be exposed to the possibility of owning a slice of the companies they work in.

Private equity funds become ideal vehicles for such opportunities to be realised. They are unbiased financial investors that have no legacy relationships with the businesses under consideration. They strongly encourage and support management to increase profitability and are willing to provide them with a share in their success.

As regional business groups begin to redefine their strategic focus and divest non-core assets, the management of those businesses could become the ideal purchasers. They will be able to leverage their understanding of the market, the industry and its operations to ideal effect. This could be an outright purchase by the management (supported by a private equity group) or it could be a three-way process in which the management, the existing owners and a private equity group combine in a partnership structure to participate jointly in the risks and rewards that may be created.

Many expatriate-owned companies in the region are also entering a transitional phase. Typically, these businesses have been founded and run by a single individual with no long-term, natural commitment to the region. While many of these businesses have been highly successful, a significant number of the owners of such businesses are now looking to exit from their businesses in order to return to their country of origin, to address succession issues or diversify their personal holdings.

THE CHECK LIST FOR PROGRESS

A number of macro-economic factors look likely to encourage the development of private equity in the GCC. According to Start Consult, a specialist management consultancy firm, there are six core factors which will determine how successful the development of the industry really is:

- Macro-economic conditions: can the countries of the GCC maintain their stable growth rates and high levels of GDP per capita?

- Regulatory infrastructure: what initiatives will governments implement to improve the regulatory framework in this emerging market?
- Availability of quality opportunities: with so much capital returning to the region, post-9/11, will there be enough suitable investments?
- Economic restructuring: some countries in the region are undergoing economic liberalisation to enhance the private sector's role in economic growth.
- Human capital: there is a general shortage of skilled, educated labour in the region. Nevertheless some countries are taking steps to create an environment that might attract such human capital. Alternatively, they are beginning to cultivate local resources.
- Exit mechanism: capital markets in the region lack depth and liquidity, and merger and acquisition activity has been low in recent years. However, there are a number of serious initiatives in the region intended to facilitate the development of capital markets. In addition, trade sales offer an excellent exit route for private equity transactions in the region.

The Gulf always seems to be on fast-forward. Visitors who spend any length of time in the region return home rapidly bemused at the slothfulness of their home country. Even London seems slow in comparison with what is being constructed in Qatar or Dubai.

The Gulf will continue to flourish as an economic region and it is likely that private equity will play an increasingly key role in this prosperity. This should have a knock-on effect, whereby a few successes in the region will encourage local and international players to enter the markets.

This would be healthy, since competition would benefit the entire industry. As Arif Naqvi points out: "The industry growing collectively will be the best outcome for everyone going forward."

Guy Hands, chief executive of leading private equity firm Terra Firma Capital Partners, says: "If I was starting out in private equity today, the possibility of high returns in this region would be very attractive. I believe passionately that private equity can transform an economy."

The economies of the Gulf States are now ready for that transformation. Arif Naqvi talks of a region at an "inflexion point ... the likes of which have not been seen since the end of the First World War. Never before has there been such a compelling argument for private equity deployment." Naqvi makes no disguise of his call to arms: "The view from my window in the Emirates Tower is no different from the skyline in Frankfurt ... everyone needs to recognise their role in elevating this region to where it could be and where it should be."

However the distinction needs to be made between the Gulf, which is racing ahead courtesy of high oil prices and a supportive political environment, and the rest of the Levant region. More opportunities might exist in the likes of Lebanon, Jordan and Morocco but they are harder to complete as the markets are more underdeveloped than the neighbouring Gulf.

Of course, private equity alone is not sufficient to stimulate an economy – indeed it would be unhealthy if too much emphasis were placed on its capabilities. As Mario Giannini, chief executive of the financial institution Hamilton Lane, points out: "Our sole criterion is return. Clients get nervous if they hear that private equity is being used for alternative goals." He is absolutely right. Nonetheless, it is clear that the private equity industry has a vital role to play in the Gulf and the Levant.

David Jackson, executive vice-president at Istithmar, says: "I doubt that the people at Blackstone sat around waiting for things to happen." Vast amounts of capital have been repatriated to the Gulf. Even if oil prices drop and some of that capital is reinvested abroad, the seed has now been sown.

Arab investors have woken up to the vast possibilities in the region. They are unlikely to drift back to sleep again. The private equity juggernaut is gaining momentum and will become a key force to be reckoned with throughout the region over the coming decades.

Appendix A
Key trends for private equity professionals

i. THE IMPORTANCE OF ACTIVE OWNERSHIP

Industries cannot grow as fast as private equity has done without changing; and the 21st century private equity sector is a rather different beast from its predecessors. It has developed a new spirit and approach, most easily described as active ownership. What this means is that private equity firms have to work harder than they used to in order to generate the returns they need.

Active ownership distinguishes private equity investors from most of the institutions that put their capital in public companies. The investment world is still filled with many fund managers who take a passive approach towards the companies they own. Investors invest and a manager manages, is the old adage, and in a majority of cases it still applies. Some investors, such as Warren Buffett in the US or Hermes in the UK, become involved in their investments, but most fund managers are stock pickers first and foremost. They do not become actively focused on the day-to-day strategic development of the businesses they back.

Henry Kravis, a co-founder of KKR, sums up his version of active ownership: "We need to start adding value the day after we complete the transaction and keep working at it until the day we exit."

Recent research from management consultancy firm McKinsey suggested that if private equity firms take five specific steps to direct the companies in which they invest, these companies will almost certainly outperform their industry peers.

To compile its research, McKinsey looked at 11 leading private equity firms, all boasting better-than-average track records. Each of them submitted five or six deals from which they had exited. The deals represented a range of returns from average to very good and McKinsey then calculated the value generated by active ownership by building a model to isolate the source of each deal's value.

The model took into consideration overall stock market appreciation, sector appreciation, the effect of extra financial leverage on those market or sector gains, arbitrage (a below-market purchase price), or company out-performance. The work unearthed some fascinating findings.

- First, successful deal partners seek out expertise before committing themselves. In 83 per cent of the best deals, the initial step for investors was to secure privileged knowledge: insights from the board, management, or a trusted external source. In the worst third of deals, expertise was sought less than half of the time.

- Second, successful deal partners institute substantial and focused performance incentives – usually offering company managers 15 to 20 per cent of the total equity. Such incentives heavily target a company's leading managers, as well as a handful of others who report directly to the chief executive. In addition, successful private equity firms make it a requirement that chief executives invest personally in their ventures. There is no standard formula, but the most successful arrangements call for a significant commitment by chief executives, while ensuring that the potential rewards do not make them too risk averse.

- Next, successful private equity firms design better value creation plans and execute them more effectively. Naturally, management's input is a part of the process, but the best new owners view it with some scepticism and develop their own well-researched viewpoint that they use to challenge it. Once developed, the plan is subject to frequent review and revision, and an appropriate set of key performance indicators is developed to ensure that it remains on track. Firms implemented such a performance-management system in 92 per cent of the best-performing deals and only half as often in the worst.

- Fourth, the most effective investors simply devote more hours to the initial stages of their deals. In the best-performing ones, the partners spent more than half their time on the company during the first 100 days and met almost daily with top executives. These meetings are critical in helping key players reach a consensus on the company's strategic priorities: relationships are built and personal responsibilities detailed. Private equity firms may use the meetings to challenge management's assumptions and to unearth the company's real sources of value. By contrast, lower-performing deals typically took up only 20 per cent of investors' time during this crucial period.

- Last, if leading deal partners want to change a company's management, they do so early in the investment. In 83 per cent of the best deals – but only 33 percent of the worst – firms strengthened the management team before the closing. Later in the deal's life, the more successful deal partners are more likely to use external support to complement management than are the less successful deal partners.

These research findings pinpoint the practices that distinguish great deals from good ones. The five steps are, in the main, uncontroversial and most private equity firms believe that they abide by them. Application, however, is inconsistent and implementation seems to depend on the individual partner's beliefs and skills. Over the next few years, this is likely to change. The growing competitiveness of the industry and the increased demands of its investors mean that a more standard active-ownership process is almost certain to become *de rigueur* in times ahead.

ii. THE CHANGING DYNAMICS OF THE JOB IN 2006

As we discuss above, the skills and output required to succeed in the industry have changed dramatically in the past two decades. In the 1980s, the principal skills were financial engineering and ability to access capital. Companies were backed by private equity investors who used huge amounts of debt to fund their investments, sometimes more than 90 per cent of the acquisition price.

During the 1980s, high inflation enabled companies to increase their prices and generate more than enough cash to pay down the debt that had been put on their balance sheets to fund the acquisitions. Many of these companies were then able to float on the booming stock market at a higher multiple of underlying profits than they had been bought for. This phenomenon, known as multiple arbitrage, was a key driver of the spectacular returns that limited partners received.

In today's more sophisticated environment multiple arbitrage has become more difficult and the emphasis is on creating value through strategic growth and operational improvements. As we discuss above, successful private equity firms have moved away from being financial engineers – though this is a skill set they both retain and buy in from investment banks – to becoming active owners with operational expertise.

So today's general partner practitioners are directly involved in the sourcing of investment opportunities, the negotiation of investments into portfolio companies, the determination of their strategies, the appointment of key executives for the companies they back, the governance of their investments and finally their successful exit.

Twenty years ago it was possible for the industry's protagonists to multi-skill and achieve success. Today it is just not possible and the management companies have evolved to become machines which ensure they can compete effectively. "The most important part of my role is HR. Getting the right people both inside Terra Firma and in our investments is key to our success," says Guy Hands.

This viewpoint is shared by Arif Naqvi, the founder of Dubai-based Abraaj Capital. "There is fund-raising, deal-sourcing, screening, structuring, portfolio management and exit. Twenty years ago it was possible to spin plates and get results. But not today. You need specialists," says Naqvi.

1. Fund raising and syndication: No investments can be made if there is no fund from which to invest. The ability to raise money is therefore fundamental to the success and longevity of a franchise. US private equity giant Carlyle currently has 23 funds in its portfolio, each of which needs capital. As the industry becomes increasingly influential, courting investors will become an ever more important role and firms will be forced to develop ever more bespoke reporting documentation for investors.

2. Deal sourcing: No investments can be made unless a firm is able to pinpoint the companies in which it would like to invest. Today this means thinking strategically about key sectors and markets and then communicating that focus to intermediaries and vendors. The art of deal origination used to be little more than a black book of contacts for the key figures in a fund. Today it involves sophisticated customer relationship management (CRM) systems and military-style campaigns to win over vendors.

3. Screening and selection: Before even completing a deal, private equity investors will have produced an up-to-date business plan to cover the period in which they will invest in the company. The business plan will analyse in depth the strategic drivers of the sector in which the business operates, review the skills of the management team and provide an outline explanation of the exit strategy for the business.

This investigation of every aspect of the transaction is known as due diligence. Traditionally, due diligence has focused on legal and financial angles, checking that contracts are watertight, the ownership status of property (both physical and intellectual) stacks up and the numbers make sense. Nowadays, the remit of due diligence is much wider and external experts are brought in to assess markets, competitors, management, insurance and risk management, environmental impact and pensions.

Before any acquisition is completed, a considerable amount of time is dedicated to developing a post-acquisition strategy. The private equity team works closely with the management of portfolio companies to identify, develop and execute initiatives that enhance value, increase market share, strengthen product position or create economies of scale. One of the advantages of private equity shareholders is that they have wide-ranging experience of the issues and problems that their portfolio companies might face in their quest for growth. Some of the strategies most closely followed include:

(i) Buy and build. Often a company will be acquired as a platform to buy up other companies operating in the same, or related, markets. If the portfolio company is positioned for such an opportunity, then the private equity manager is heavily involved in finding acquisition targets and evaluating them with management. The platform company is used to consolidate other industry participants in a given sector, thereby creating industry leaders with strong market positions and attractive strategic exit possibilities. As an active, involved shareholder, the private equity firm makes sure that managers focus on effectively integrating the acquisition. In recent years, private equity firms have become adept at achieving a higher success rate on acquisitions than the general corporate market, which is in no small way down to the fact that they have more experience of it.

(ii) Institutionalise internal processes and procedures. The private equity manager works closely with the senior members of the portfolio company's management team to ensure that best practices and processes are adopted. The manager uses global benchmarks and his firm's expertise to make certain that global compliance and risk management measures are in place. Many private equity firms look to bring in established and recognised managerial disciplines, such as the Six Sigma approach pioneered by GE.

iii) Incentivisation of management. Private equity firms often implement incentive plans based on specific parameters that they have identified as areas of improvement. These could include day's receivable targets, overheads as a percentage of revenue, cash flow targets, gross margins and others. Bonuses are also introduced, based on broader net income and revenue targets. An employee stock options plan is often initiated too. Aligning the interests of employees, both senior and junior, has proved to be a significant driver of value creation.

iv) Regional expansion. Private equity firms provide portfolio companies with access to vast regional networks and help them team up with the right partners in every country. This can help companies enter new markets or source products from lower cost countries. Again, the experience gained from other companies in the portfolio means that common mistakes can be avoided.

4. *Structuring and execution:* Financing remains as important as ever. But the focus is on structuring the debt that the company takes on so that it will not be too much of a burden. The practice of financing acquisitions with more than 90 per cent debt seen in the late 1980s has long gone, and today even the most highly leveraged transactions have at least 30 per cent equity funding.

5. *Portfolio management:* Once a company has been backed by a private equity investor, it becomes subject to the individual portfolio management techniques deployed by a firm. Portfolio investments are monitored through both a formal and informal process.

The formal process includes monthly, quarterly and annual financial and management reports, showing actual performance versus budget, plan and/or projection. There are also board meetings and management meetings.

Monthly meetings
These discuss:
- Reviews of individual portfolio companies with an emphasis on management accounts.
- Analysis of individual investment risk and performance ratings; analysis of appropriate industry, sector, geographic and other pertinent concentrations.
- Assessment of all factors relative to post-acquisition strategies and plans.
- Revision of the review process if necessary.

Quarterly portfolio reports
These provide:
- Portfolio reports containing cost analyses, carrying values, estimated fair values, valuation discounts, and other factors summarising the status of individual investments.
- Documentation of any departures from or variations to post-acquisitions plans, policies and procedures and management reporting.
- Review of reports by senior management to assess current positions and develop action plans if required.

Quarterly portfolio performance
This gives details of:
- Performance reports on every fund summarising the overall position of each fund.
- Clear statement of management fees, profit share and carried interest paid to the general partner.
- Clear statement of related party transactions, benefits and fees, broken down into principal categories.
- Complete reports that are ready for distribution to limited partners.

Annual Review
This provides:
- Collation of all feedback from monthly and quarterly reports to create an extensive annual performance review.
- It includes the financial and management performance of portfolio companies and forecasts, other key performance metrics and relevant items, including current and future plans.
- The review revisits and assesses exit strategies for each investment, both primary and contingent, and modifies them if necessary.

Henry Kravis has famously described his job today in the following terms: "We only make money because we improve operations of the newly acquired company. As a result, we have had to get more skilled at building businesses. And it is no small irony that our need to work harder today to increase the value of our companies is the fault of our own collective success."

6. Exit: When and how to exit an investment is arguably the most important decision that a private equity practitioner can make. Sell too soon and you risk failing to achieve the true valuation; leave it too late and you might miss the high point. Exit plans are debated via:
- Ad hoc but frequent meetings with management, market intelligence and third party information about the company and its position.
- Meetings to determine how hands-on the private equity manager needs to be to add value to a portfolio company.
- Meetings to determine how value can be added.

iii. THE WAR FOR TALENT

Although competition within the industry has become more ferocious than ever before, many practitioners view this as evidence of the sector's coming of age. Indeed the ability of private equity to attract talent is further proof of its increasing importance within the financial markets. Jack Welch was arguably the world's most respected business leader when he was at GE. Where is he now? He works for Clayton, Dubilier & Rice, a leading US private equity fund.

His principle focus is to conduct quarterly performance reviews with each chief executive in the portfolio. The prospect of being grilled on decisions taken in the past quarter and what you intend to do in the next one by the world's leading businessman is expected to improve returns. It will undoubtedly be a useful marketing tool as well in the winning of competitive deals for CDR.

"Today I see private equity as about as much fun as you can have if you like managing, improving assets, building leadership teams, which is what we do at CDR," says Welch. He is not alone. Lou Gerstner, architect of the IBN turnaround, is chairman of Carlyle.

It used to be the case that Fortune 500, CAC 40 and FTSE 100 boardrooms were the natural habitat for outstanding business leaders. They may still be. But the rewards on offer in private equity, coupled with its ability to operate outside the glare of the public company spotlight, make it an increasingly attractive destination for some of the smartest minds in business.

In Goldman Sachs, the culture of success, author Lisa Endlich ascribes part of the bank's incredible achievement to "the edge" it receives from being "at the nexus" of advising governments and major businesses. While Goldman's business was built on advising and trading, and is therefore rather different from private equity firms, certain similarities apply.

For something unusual is taking place inside the world's leading private equity firms. They are getting ever more confident in their ability to hire individuals with extensive political experience or with brilliant operational backgrounds.

John Major, the former British Prime Minister, was until recently on the payroll at Carlyle, as is Arthur Levitt, a former chairman of America's Securities & Exchange Commission. These individuals are able to distil their wisdom and help the funds they work with on a part-time basis.

Of equal note are the changes emerging in the way investment teams are structured. In the early to mid-1980s the industry sought out corporate financiers and debt architects to develop business models that would enable them to achieve the appropriate returns. Being able to understand balance sheets and financing structures remains vitally important. But so is having industry and operational experience, blended with a deeply analytical approach to what is going on in a sector and a market.

According to the "New Kings of Capitalism" survey by The Economist in November 2004, KKR borrowed 97 per cent of the $4.8billion cost for its investment in America's Safeway supermarket chain in 1986. Today the debt-equity ratio is much lower, with most deals built around an expectation that a fund will invest up to one-third of the price in equity, relying on the debt markets to fund the remaining two-thirds.

So those financial engineering skills, while relevant, are just not as important today: the skill-set has become much more operationally focused.

Successful private equity practitioners invest large quantities of time in defining the anticipated strategy of their investments long before they take control. They develop 100-day plans, one-year outlines and exit strategies for their investments long before they have ever signed the cheque to make the original investment. Depth of approach and rigour lie behind the out-performance of parts of the private equity asset class.

Max Burger-Calderon, a senior partner and chairman of Asia for Apax Partners Worldwide, says: "The more professional you are, the better. It is about doing something every day well. A professional is always up there and that is exactly what you have to be. That is hard to deliver. It starts at 7am and goes on till midnight."

It is subsequently argued in this book that private equity can be a definitive long-term means of creating sustained performance and shareholder value for businesses in the Middle East. To truly achieve this will take a huge effort on the part of all those involved in the region, as Burger-Calderon suggests.

iv. THE AVAILABLE REWARDS

The rewards for those who have been successful have been truly incredible. According to Private Equity Intelligence, a data provider which examined returns from funds invested between 1991 and 2005, investors will end up sharing profits of $1 trillion (€830billion). It has calculated that pension funds, insurance companies and wealthy individuals might receive more than $750billion in returns. The rest? That is likely to be shared between the general partners – the individuals inside the funds who are making the investment decisions.

Mark O'Hare, managing director of PEI and an author of the report, says: "If this was a sealed market, you would have to say that too much money is coming in and returns are not sustainable. But it is not sealed – more public companies will go private and the industry is always looking for new ways to add value."

PEI's calculations are based on a number of assumptions – primarily because most of the funds raised by the industry in 2004 and 2005 are yet to be called up and little money has been invested or realised. O'Hare says: "We assume that all available money gets called up, but that there is no further improvement in the vintages from 1997 to 2000, although there probably will be. These are conservative assumptions."

The returns have been based on a stable and improving global economic environment, a downward trend in global interest rates and an expanding global market created by the end of the Cold War. Those ideal conditions are unlikely to be repeated, but there is no reason to think that returns will collapse.

No wonder individuals such as Guy Hands of Terra Firma, David Rubinstein of Carlyle and Steve Schwarzman of Blackstone have become pin-ups for today's MBA students, who all want to replicate their success and enjoy their wealth.

Meanwhile there are also rewards available for those who find themselves executives of private equity-backed companies. According to a recent report by professional services firm Deloitte, the median pay (including salary, annual bonus and share schemes) of an executive at a FTSE 100 company is around £1.5 million. Deloitte looked at companies floating on the London Stock

Exchange – a large proportion of which are backed by private equity funds – and found that the median shareholding of a full-time executive was 11 per cent, with a value of £7 million.
Roll in the fact that the public company executive's remuneration will be taxed as income at around 40 per cent, whereas the shares held in a private equity environment will be taxed on sale as capital gains at an effective rate of 10 per cent, and it is easy to see why more and more executives are taking the private option.

There is, though, a downside that is also at the heart of how private equity functions. In return for the opportunity to make themselves fabulously rich, the executive is required to invest a substantial amount of their own personal wealth in the venture. There are no hard and fast rules about how much but it is generally accepted that the sum needs to be significant enough to "hurt" if the money is lost.

The logic here is straightforward and the industry term for it is "alignment of interest". This extends beyond the portfolio company level to the way the funds themselves are structured. For example, when a private equity firm raises money from its investors (usually called limited partners), then the partners in that firm are required to invest their own money in the fund as well. Standard practice is for these partners to contribute at least two per cent of the targeted amount.

Similar rationale underpins the remuneration paid to executives within the private equity fund. They are paid salaries that are way above national averages but, relative to other executives in the world of finance, they are significantly below what might be expected. Where the real reward comes is in carried interest. Once a fund has exceeded a targeted rate of return (known as a hurdle), then a percentage of the gain, commonly 20 per cent, but as much as 30 per cent for the best Silicon Valley venture capitalists, is shared out amongst the firm's partners. Again, this is a powerful incentive for them to drive value from their investments and generate a good return for their investors. It is worth pointing out that this reward only crystallises when investments are sold on for a profit. But when this works, it can work phenomenally well. It has been reported that the seven partners in Benchmark Capital, a Menlo Park venture capital firm, reaped $150 million each from the sale of its stake in online auction provider eBay.

v. CORPORATE GOVERNANCE IN PRIVATE EQUITY: LEADERS OR LAGGARDS?

Private equity's collective success story can be attributed to many factors, but there is little doubt that the industry's approach to corporate governance has played a part in its success. Private equity firms are so operationally focused on the strategy, performance and outcome of their investments that they view the management of their portfolio company's boards as a matter of paramount importance. Corporate governance problems are either extremely well hidden or genuinely rare in private equity.

Henry Kravis describes the maximisation of shareholder value as one of his key enduring values on which KKR has been built. "Most of us in the industry have always held seats on our portfolio companies' boards of directors. But we generally aren't board members who show up once a month and whose primary source of revenue is elsewhere. Most of us in the industry live with these businesses on a day-to-day basis as shareholders and as guardians of our limited partners' capital. We perform extensive due diligence and analysis, not only of the businesses in which we invest, but also of their competitors and the overall industry dynamics. We at KKR, like many others in our industry, I am sure, are very granular in our approach to monitoring a business."

What that means in practice is that private equity funds should and do know their portfolios very well, in some instances, better than the management teams. "We have a laser focus on the bottom line. Board meetings are interactive discussions, not reports to passive, friendly directors. All decisions are made with a clear intent to create shareholder value. And while each private equity firm has its particular strengths, I believe that, as an industry, we have always strived for transparency to protect the shareholders," says Kravis.

Transparency is a topic of some controversy in today's financial markets. As the industry becomes more and more high profile, there are increasing calls for it to be more open about the way it conducts itself and the money made by the limited partners and the companies in which they invest. This issue is just one of the challenges faced by the industry in 2006 and beyond.

vi. THE MCKINSEY PERSPECTIVE: THE NECESSARY SKILLS TO SUCCEED

Conor Kehoe, founder and director of McKinsey's private equity practice in Europe, believes that successful private equity firms can be defined by their approach to six key areas:

- Deal insights
- The amount of time a partner spends on a deal
- The value assertion plan
- The approach to management change
- The approach to incentives
- External support

In each of these fields, McKinsey differentiates between "common practice" and "best practice".

Where common practice is satisfied with a simple due diligence approach, best practice is more likely to garner insight from alternative experts. Common practice tends to focus on the chief executive of an investee company and due diligence will take up only 15 per cent of a private equity partner's time; best practice will focus across the board and constitute nearer 45 per cent of the partner's time. Common practice will review a value creation plan; best practice will create a new one. Common practice will consider the board in any management changes; best practice will recruit new management, where necessary. Common practice will spread equity widely; best practice will restrict equity incentives to top managers only. Common practice will use external support all too infrequently; best practice will do the opposite.

Christopher O'Brien, head of Direct Investment at Investcorp, provides an equally coherent list defined as "The basic principles of private equity investing" and divided between dos and don'ts.

- Do adhere to investment criteria; buy businesses you understand; diversify in a disciplined fashion and buy industry or product leaders. Don't attempt venture capital type bets; lose your discipline on price; and target industries under continuing price pressure. Put more simplistically, O'Brien's maxims can be summarised as: "Buy the right business at the right time, add value and sell opportunistically."

The private equity team at KPMG also identifies five key stages at which it is vital for private equity firms to operate good corporate governance: fundraising; deal origination; investment appraisal; active management; and value realisation. In other words, at every stage of the private equity process.

At the fundraising stage, KPMG asserts that it is vital to know your existing investors and engage in open communication. Once deals are being sourced, it is important to maintain deal flow. When it comes to investment appraisal, the firm must focus on its conversion rate. A good private equity company might receive 100 proposals per month, which will have to be whittled down to an initial ten and then ultimately two or three. An investment committee with clear requirements will be appointed and due diligence will be carried out conscientiously.

The ultimate decision on whether to buy or stay away cannot be made until all these factors have been considered. At the active management stage, the critical success factors will be the requisite access to appropriate skills and the courage to take the right decisions. Ultimately, a successful fund will be confident of prioritising exit strategies to generate maximum returns.

Appendix B
List of private equity operators

The following is a contemporary list of private equity operators that are focused on investing in companies in the Middle East. The list is focused on the management companies as opposed to individual funds. In certain instances a single management company might oversee a number of funds, such as Abraaj Capital, whilst in other instances start-up management companies will only have one fund.

BAHRAIN
Name: Gulf Finance House (Bahrain)
Founded: 1999 - listed on the Bahrain and Kuwait stock exchange
Funds under management: Paid up capital of $300m
Contact: www.gfhouse.com

Name: Islamic Development Bank Infrastructure Fund
Founded: 2001
Funds under management: $1.5bn
Contact: www.isdb.org/english_docs/fund_home

EGYPT
Name: Citadel Capital
Contact: www.citadelcapital.com.eg

Name: EFG Hermes
Founded: 1980
Funds under management: US$ 470m
Contact: www.efg-hermes.com/business_lines/privateequity/default.aspx

Name: IT Ventures
Founded: 2003
Funds under management: IT Ventures $150m

Name: Concord International Investments
Founded: 1995
Funds under management: Concord International Investments and Credit Suisse have formed a private banking joint venture in Egypt. The two companies have formed Swiss Egyptian Portfolio Management.
Contact: ciie@concord.com.eg

IRAQ
Name: Daman Asset Management
Founded: 2003
Funds under management: $50m
Contact: www.daman.ae

JORDAN
Name: Atlas Investments (Amman)
Founded: 2002
Funds under management: The Jordan Fund $50m
Contact: www.atlasinvest.net

Name: Catalyst Private Equity
Founded: 2005
Funds under management: Catalyst Technology Fund

Name: Foursan Group
Founded: 2000
Funds under management: $50m
Contact: www.4san.com

Name: Technology Accelerator Fund
Founded: 2005
Funds under management: Accelerator Technology Fund $50m

KUWAIT
Name: Global Investment House
Founded: 1998
Funds under management: KD 1.7bn
Contact: www.globalinv.net

Name: Khazaen Venture Capital
Founded: 2005
Funds under management: Khazaen Venture Capital $25m
Contact: http://khazaen.com

Name: Kipco Asset Management Company (Kuwait)
Founded: 1998
Funds under management: KD 1.3bn
Contact: www.kamconline.com

Name: Markaz
Founded: 2003
Funds under management: $3.5bn
Contact: www.markaz.com

Name: National Technology Enterprises Company
Founded: 2005
Funds under management: National Technology Enterprises Company NTEC $330m

LEBANON
Name: Byblos Bank
Founded: 2006
Funds under management: $4bn
Contact: www.byblosbank.com.lb

Name: Capital Trust Group
Founded: 1985-Middle East Office incorporated in 2004
Funds under management: No details
Contact: Tel +965 240-6340

Name: Eagle Management
Founded: 2002
Funds under management: Eagle One Real Estate Investment Company (Holding) $12m
Contact: Saradar Investment House, www.investhouse.com

Name: Middle East Capital Group
Founded: 1996
Funds under management: Lebanon Real Estate Development Fund
Contact: www.mecg.com.lb

MOROCCO
Name: Atlamed SA (Morocco)
Founded: 2005
Funds under management: Atlamed Invest $60m
Contact: http://www.eib.eu.int/projects/pipeline/project.asp?pipe=1304&listing=1

SAUDI ARABIA
Name: Swicorp
Founded: 1987
Funds under management:
(i) Launched MENA Water Ventures with Danone in 2003
(ii) Intaj Capital $60m first closing, rising to $200m in 2006
Contact: www.swicorp.com

TUNISIA

Name: Tuninvest (Societe Tunisienne d'Investissement a Capital Risque)
Founded: 1994
Funds under management: Six funds from 1994 all with circa $8m
Contact: www.tuninvest.com

UAE

Name: Abraaj Capital (Dubai)
Founded: 2002
Funds under management:
(i) Abraaj Buyout Fund LP was the first Middle East focused buyout fund. Closed in June 2003 with total commitments of US$116m
(ii) The Abraaj Real Estate Fund LP. The Fund was oversubscribed beyond the US$100m target capitalisation. Launched in June 2004, it closed earlier than the planned date of December 31, 2004 due to large investor response.
(iii) The Abraaj Special Opportunities Fund LP. The Fund closed on December 31, 2003 with total commitments of US$32.55m.
Contact: www.abraaj.com

Name: Abu Dhabi Investment House
Founded: 2006
Funds under management: For 2006 Al Arabi PE Fund $75m
Contact: +971 2-681-1233

Name: Dubai International Capital (part of Dubai Holding)
Founded: October 26 2004
Funds under management: JD Capital £272m
Contact: www.dubaiic.com

Name: Evolence Capital
Founded: May 2002
Funds under management: BTU Fund $300m
Contact: www.evolvence.com

Name: GCC Energy Fund Managers
Founded: 2005
Funds under management: GCC Energy Fund $300m
Contact: www.globalinv.net

Name: HSBC Private Equity Middle East Management
Founded: 1975
Funds under management: HSBC PE Ltd Middle East $118m
Contact: hibme@emirates.net.ae

Name: Injazat Technology Fund (Dubai)
Founded: 2001
Funds under management: Shari'ah compliant venture capital fund $50m
Contact: www.injazatfund.com

Name: Istithmar (Dubai govt institution)
Founded:
Funds under management: No details
Contact: www.istithmar.ae

Name: Ithmar Capital
Founded: 2004
Funds under management: Ithmar Fund 1 $70m
Contact: www.ithmar.com

Name: National Investor
Founded: 1994
Funds under management: Paid up capital $136m
Contact: www.nationalinvestor.ae

Name: Shuaa Partners (Dubai which used to be the Arabian General Investment Corporation)
Founded: 1979
Funds under management:
(i) 1998 co manages $50m MENAVEST fund with Capital Trust Group
(ii) Paid up capital of $150 including a US60m rights issue
Contacts: www.shuaacapital.com

Name: Weather Investments
Funds under management: No details
Founded: 1997
Contacts: www.otelecom.com

Sources

I am particularly grateful to the following people for all their help and assistance.

Fawaz Al Alamy (Ministry of Commerce and Industry, Saudi Arabia)
Sameer Al Ansari (DIC)
Khaled Bin Zayed Al Nahayan (Bin Zayed)
Sheikh Sultan Bin Saqr Al Qassami (GIBCA)
Ahmad Mohammad Al Sari (Malaz Group)
Abdulmohsen Al Touq (Al Touq)
Bassam Al Awadallah (Abdullah II Fund for Development)

Khalid Abdulla-Janahi (Shamil Bank)
Khalid Abunayyan (Abunayyan Trading Corp)
Samer Alhaj (Gulf Investment House)
Nicholas Ashby (Celadon Capital)
Ayman Arekat (World Capital Partners)
Deepak Atal (Ominvest)
Mahmoud Atalla (HSBC)

Rami Bazzi (Injazat Fund)
Faisal Bin Juma Belhoul (Ithmar)
Avi Bhorjani (Bates Pan Gulf)
Brad Bourland (SAMBA)
Max Burger-Calderon (Apax)

Edwin Charnaud (Marsh)
Mohammed Chowdhury (Arcapita)
Sherard Cowper-Coles (HM Ambassador to Saudi Arabia)
Jeremy Coller (Coller Capital)

Dr Abdallah E Dabbagh (Ma'aden)
Ashish Dave (KPMG)
Iyad Duwaji (Shuaa Capital)

Mohammed Elahi (Andes Capital Group)
Hassan Elkhatib (EFG Hermes)
Yasser El Mallawany (EFG Hermes)

Prince Fahad Bin Abdullah (Saudi Arabia)
Samir Fancy (Renaissance Services)

Shafik Gabr (ARTOC)
Fadi Ghandour (Aramex)
Imad Ghandour (Gulf Capital)

Saed Ahmed Ghobash (Ghobash Trading and Investing)

Jonathan Hall (Abraaj Capital)
Mazen Hayek (MS&L)
Hassan Heikal (EFG Hermes)
John Hobday (Citigate Incepta Middle East)
David Hodgkinson (HSBC)
Sameer Huda (Hadef Al Dhahiri & Associates)
Imtiaz Hydari (HBG Holdings)
Alan Hyslop (Dubai International Capital)

Ihsan Jawad (Zawya)
Abdulaziz A Jazzar (Malaz)
Ali Mohammed Juma (Vision Investment Services)

Saud Abdulaziz Kanoo (Ossis Property Developers)
Makram Kubeisy (Shuaa Capital)
Suresh Kumar (Emirates Bank)

Roger Leeds (EMPEA)
Anoosha Livani (Kleinwort Capital)

Leith Masri (Foursan)
Michael McDaniel (Dubai Aluminium)
Murtaza Merchant (IFI)
Azmi Mikati (Investcom)
Charles Milner (KPMG)
Abhinav Munshi (Abraaj Capital)
Graeme Muir (Norton Rose)

Anil Nahar (Bahwan Engineering Company)
Arif Naqvi (Abraaj Capital)

David Price (HSBC)

Edward Quinlan (Ernst & Young)

Raj Rajagopalan (Emirates Financial Services)
Rachid Mohammed Rachid

Abe Saad (Shuaa)
Shirish Saraf (Abraaj Capital)
John Sfakianakis (SAMBA)
Waqar Siddique (Abraaj Capital)

Humayun Shahryar (Abraaj Capital)
Laila Shaker (ARTOC)
Khaled Sheta (International Group of Investments)
Frederic Sicre (Abraaj Capital)
Zafar Siddiqi (CNBC)
Dr Karim El Solh (Gulf Capital)
Tom Speechley (Macfarlanes)

Khaldoon Tabaza (Riyada Ventures)
Colin Taylor (CSFB)
Adil Toubia (GCC Energy)

Arif Usmani (SAMBA)

Christopher Welch (Meketa Investment Group)

Azhar Zafar (Ernst & Young)

There are five other people who only agreed to be interviewed on the promise that no one would ever know they were involved. Thank you in particular to Mr S who gave me the inspiration for my First Impressions, and to ON for introducing me to the region.

I am also keen to reference a small number of books and publications that helped my understanding of the region and the protagonists operating inside it.

The Merchants – The Big Business Families of Saudi Arabia and the Gulf States by Michael Field (1985)

A MEED Practical & Business Guide to the UAE-7th Edition, MEED (2004)

Private Equity – Examining the new conglomerates of European Business by Peter Temple (1988)

Across the Generations – Insights from 100-Year-Old Businesses, BDO Stoy Hayward Centre for Family Businesses (2004)

Venture Capital & Private Equity, A Casebook, Josh Lerner, FT Prentice Hall (2004)

Why some private equity firms do better than others, McKinsey Quarterly (2005: 1)

Investments don't govern themselves: Active ownership is the answer, McKinsey Quarterly (2005: 2)

Finally I have made use of Zawya, the business news service, supplements from the Financial Times and articles from a host of international and regional newspapers and magazines to inform my knowledge. These publications include Private Equity International, The Banker Magazine Middle East, MEED, Gulf Business, Arabian Business and a raft of local newspapers.